Delere Press
The Screaming Series

SERIES EDITOR
LIM LEE CHING

THIS PAPERBACK EDITION FIRST
PUBLISHED IN 2018 BY DELERE
PRESS LLP, AS PART OF THE
SCREAMING SERIES.

ANYTHING YOU CAN GET
AWAY WITH: CREATIVE
PRACTICES
© EDDIE TAY
© EVA LEUNG

FIRST PUBLISHED IN 2018 BY
DELERE PRESS LLP
WWW.DELEREPRESS.COM
DELERE PRESS LLP REG NO.
T11LL1061K

ISBN 978-981-11-7912-9

ANYTHING YOU CAN GET AWAY WITH: CREATIVE PRACTICES

ANYTHING YOU CAN GET AWAY WITH: CREATIVE PRACTICES

EDDIE TAY

Delere Press

This book is published with the support of the Publication Subvention Fund for 2017-2018 provided by the Faculty of Arts, Chinese University of Hong Kong.

Early versions of the chapters have been previously published as follows:

"Writing Photography, Seeing Poetry and Creative Writing Scholarship". *New Writing: The International Journal for the Theory and Practice of Creative Writing*, 13.3 (2016): 387-401.

"Superficiality, Mythification, and Irreality: Towards a Writing Practice". *New Ideas in the Writing Arts*. Ed. Graeme Harper. Newcastle upon Tyne, United Kingdom: Cambridge Scholars Publishing, 2013. pp.113-126.

"Multiculturalisms, Mistranslations and Bilingual Poetry: On Writing as a Chinese". *New Writing: The International Journal for the Theory and Practice of Creative Writing*, 6:1 (2009): 5-14.

(with Eva Leung as second author) "On Learning, Teaching and the Pursuit of Creative Writing in Singapore and Hong Kong". *New Writing: The International Journal for the Theory and Practice of Creative Writing*, 8:2 (2011): 103-113. Article supported by CUHK's Direct Grant for Research.

"Curriculum as Cultural Critique: Creative Writing Pedagogy in Hong Kong". Ed. Dan Disney. *Exploring Second Language Creative Writing: Beyond Babel*. Philadelphia, USA: John Benjamins Publishing Company, 2014. 103-118.

"On Places and Spaces: The Possibilities of Teaching Arthur Yap". *Common Lines and City Spaces: A Critical Anthology on Arthur Yap*. Ed. Gui Weihsin. Singapore: Institute of Southeast Asian Studies, 2014. 96-113.

"The Poetics of Occupy Central – A Photo Essay". A plenary talk. *Imagining Asia Symposium*. Organised by College of Humanities, Arts, and Social Sciences, Nanyang Technological University. 16-18 Jan 2015. Subsequently published as "The Poetics of the Umbrella Movement" in *Cha: An Asian Literary Journal*. Issue 29, Sept 2015. [http://www.asiancha.com/content/view/2199/117/]

"Street Meditations: On Poetry, Street Photography and Everyday Life in Hong Kong". *Asiatic*, Vol. 6 Number 2. Dec 2012. pp. 31-44.

My gratitude to Lim Lee Ching, who edited this book. Many thanks also to Jeremy Fernando, for believing.

PREVIOUS BOOKS BY THE SAME AUTHOR

Dreaming Cities. Singapore: Math Paper Press, 2016.
Poetry and street photography collection.

Colony, Nation, and Globalisation:
Not at Home in Singaporean and Malaysian Literature.
Hong Kong University Press, 2011; Singapore: NUS Press, 2011.
Academic monograph.

The Mental Life of Cities. Hong Kong: Chameleon Press, 2010.
Poetry collection.
Awarded Singapore Literature Prize 2012 (English Category).

A Lover's Soliloquy. Hong Kong: Sixth Finger Press, 2005.
Poetry collection, including free translations of Li Shang-yin.
Published with grant support from National Arts Council (Singapore).

Remnants. Singapore: Ethos Books, 2001.
Poetry collection, including free translations of Li Po, Tu Fu and Li Ho.
Published with grant support from National Arts Council (Singapore).

This book is dedicated to May Lyn, Titus, Tabitha, and Peggy.

CREATIVE WRITING, STREET PHOTOGRAPHY, SCHOLARSHIP

This book takes stock of the practices of writing poetry, taking street photographs and creative writing scholarship. It adopts both imaginative and critical ways of writing and exploring both texts and practices. I think of myself as a MacGyver-type character, indulging in the art of bricolage, pulling together poetry, street photography and autoethnography. Marshall McLuhan once wrote that "[a] rt is anything you can get away with" (*Medium is the Massage* 132-136). I am going to borrow from him and say that "scholarship is anything you can get away with". Hence, this project is a self-conscious assemblage of sorts, drawing from various genres. It is a scholarly work that draws from the methodology of autoethnography, it is a creative work to do with poetry writing, and it is a critical reflection on the possibilities of street photography. It also features my own poetry and street photography. Although I am working to articulate a socio-philosophy of creative work, teaching and scholarship situated specifically within Hong Kong and Singapore, I write with an awareness that the issues I examine here are nonetheless relevant to fellow writers and artists in other locales who are likewise searching for ways to talk about what it is that drives them.

At the same time, this book exemplifies an autoethnographic approach to understanding creative practices, teaching and scholarship. Given that I am embedded in the social phenomenon that is being observed, there is a certain amount of subjectivity as well as a feedback loop in that what one observes might constitute one's own pre-dispositions as a writer. In other words, I fully acknowledge that what is written here may in part be projections rather than impartial observations.

The critical advantages and problems associated with autoethnography as a research methodology have been discussed in various quarters. As a recognized methodology, it comprises a heterogeneous set of rival practices. We see this in the reactions to Leon Anderson's landmark paper "Analytic Autoethnography" and his responses to those reactions[1]. In their response to Anderson's paper, Carolyn S. Ellis and Arthur B. Bochner are concerned about the suppression of the personal narratives of both the observer and the observed when one privileges analysis; and they caution against being too overtly analytical to the extent that one becomes "a detached spectator" such that knowledge becomes "disembodied" (431). On the other hand, Paul Atkinson argues that there might be "the elevation

---

[1] See the entire issue of Journal of Contemporary Ethnography 35.4 (2006) for papers pertaining to the critical advantages and potential pitfalls of analytic autoethnography as a research methodology.

of the autobiographical to such a degree that the ethnographer becomes more memorable than the ethnography, the self more absorbing than other social actors" (402). Suffice to say, the main pitfall of autoethnography is self-indulgence; yet I wish to point out that it is not the case that I am offering myself as a privileged observer-participant, but that I am opening myself up to critique even as I allow myself a certain degree of self-reflexivity in writing about the cultural landscape as a social rather than as a textual landscape.

I am very conscious of the fact that most of the time, I play a dual role and am torn between two kinds of activities with very different agendas. On the one hand, as a scholar of literature, I understand post-structuralist arguments to do with the fictive nature of the self, with how identities are socially constructed. In this respect, literary works are either functions of social and very public tensions, and the self is a function of qualities and attributes to do with the conditions of textuality. Thus, Roland Barthes' "Death of the Author" thesis and Michel Foucault's arguments concerning the author-function are more or less the bedrock to understanding the conditions of textuality. On the other hand, what happens when I am doing the work of a creative writer? In this case, the author, obviously, is not dead, and I don't feel very much like an author-function.

The previous sentence is rather glib, obviously. You could say that I am an author-function right now in the sense that I am part of a larger discourse, and that you will always have to regard me as dead in the sense that my intention, biography, ethnicity, tastes, and so on could be ignored or attended to, depending on the reader's impulses; to use Barthes' words, it is not the "origin" but the "destination" of the text that should be the focus (Barthes *Image-Music-Text* 148). That is who I am for the reader or listener. But who am I for me? We've got a point-of-view problem here.

The trouble with this is that it does not help me very much when I am writing a poem or taking a photograph. The best I can do is to say I am being cunning here; even though I do honestly subscribe to the constellation of ideas to do with the text being "a tissue of quotations", the author function, the death of the author, and all that, I often find it practically convenient to suspend these ideas when I am writing (Barthes *Image-Music-Text* 146). I have to behave as if I am at the center of my work, that I am an autonomous meaning-producing agent within a larger discursive web. In this, I find comfort in what Foucault said in an interview, that we all behave as if "art is something which is specialized or done by experts who are artists. But couldn't everyone's life become a work of art?" ("On the Genealogy of Ethics" 1983/1997: 261). As he puts it, "[f]rom the…idea that the self is not given to us, [he thinks] there is only one practical consequence: we have to create ourselves as a work of art" (1983/1997: 262). Foucault who gave us the concept of the author-function also gave us a way out. Barthes may be said to have done the same; he who gave us the death-of-the-author thesis is also capable of writing of

> a discomfort [he] had always suffered from: the uneasiness of being a subject torn between two languages, one expressive, the other critical…For each time, having resorted to any such language to whatever degree, each time [he] felt it hardening and .. [he] would gently leave it and seek elsewhere: [he] began to speak differently. (Barthes *Camera Lucida* 8)

This is what I am aiming for as a creative writer-academic – to be uneasy and to speak differently from myself. This is my life project, my answer whenever someone asks me questions about my identity as an academic as opposed to my identity as a creative writer. This is a question about theory as opposed to practice, about post-structuralist thought as opposed to the Romantic imagination, and of course the question always already presumes that dichotomy between theory and practice, the sophisticated scholar as opposed to the naive poet, and so on. I am trying to create a language for myself. I am allowing language to create my self.

—

The following sums up my weekday morning routine: I wake up my son at 6.15am, make sure he has his breakfast, and then we'll go to the car at 6.45am. I'll drop him off ten minutes later at his school bus pick-up point (his school bus does not go into the slightly remote Hong Kong village where I live). I'll then drive back to the village and wait in the car for my wife and daughter. I'll then drop my daughter off at the same pick-up point (because her school day starts 40 minutes after her brother's, her school bus comes for her later). My wife and I will then proceed to the university where we both work.

Depending on which part of the semester we're in, at my office, I'll either be preparing to teach, grading essays, or writing. I'll sometimes gaze out my window, and be reminded that such a view is possible only because of various nested frames. You could say the hill is framed by the window, part of a larger office building. So from my point of view, it is the man-made and rationally-constituted environment which frames nature. On the other hand, we tend to forget that the urban environment of Hong Kong is in fact determined and constrained by its hilly natural environment:

This photograph is a visual trope concerning the nested conditions of urban necessities borne out of rational calculation and attentiveness to beauty. For me, the photograph is ironic – one looks out and away, yet in the end, one can only look at oneself. For anyone who is attuned to the inner life, there is often a dialectic between mindfulness and manic activity, between restfulness and daily routine, between aesthetics and practical necessity.

How does one cope with the demands of being an academic working in the humanities, subject to managerial and corporatist demands, to measures of productivity, impact and socio-economic relevance and, at the same time, produce work that is mindful, joyful and enabling, in other words, work that is attentive to what it means to be human? To seek to work creatively is to wrestle with the conditions of modernity, a condition that demands a routine borne out of rational calculation (hence my weekday mornings); at the same time, the very same conditions also require labor that is insightful and meaningful, a kind of labor drawn from a space outside of rational calculation. There is then a dichotomy between external demands and this "inner life" as elaborated by Georg Simmel in his 1903 essay "Metropolis and Mental Life":

> Punctuality, calculability, exactness are forced upon life by the complexity and extension of metropolitan existence and are not only most intimately connected with its money economy and intellectualist character. These traits must also color the contents of life and favor the exclusion of those irrational, instinctive, sovereign traits and impulses which aim at determining the mode of life from within, instead of receiving the general and precisely schematized form of life from without. (413)

Simmel's work is a reminder of the need for one to constantly negotiate the rationality of everyday life with those irrational impulses "from within". I find in street photography an expression of that negotiation.

In *Street Photography: From Atget to Cartier-Bresson*, Clive Scott makes a distinction between documentary photography and street photography, arguing that the latter "wills a 'poetry' into existence" (72). One may extend this distinction to say that documentary photography is to street photography what a sociologist is to a poet. The former largely proceeds with empirical observations and social categories, while the latter relies on incommensurable moments. Documentary photography usually deals with objective, social and shared truths in capital letters, such as "Third World Poverty", "World Peace", "Rampant Consumerism", and so on. In contrast, street photography is often concerned with individuals, interiorities and private epiphanies. It is concerned, in other words, with *punctum*, that which pricks me, so that I could begin to, in the words of Michel de Certeau, "articulat[e] a second, poetic geography on top of the geography of the literal, forbidden or permitted meaning" (105). I am interested in absorbing urban spaces into the mental space of creative practice, transforming everyday public scenes into an existential domain that is productive to thought, agency and meaning creation. I am not suggesting that a photograph is either a work of documentary photography or street photography. It could be both, of course. With the phrase "poetic desire", I am marking out a domain of irreverence, of playful intention and will, to do with making and reading photography.

Street photography as a genre relies on found moments. We talk about found objects in the world of art, whereby the artist makes use of readymade objects in his or her work, the most famous being Marcel Duchamp's *Fountain* which was previously a urinal. Found moments, then, represent that sort of ethos as well, in that the street photographer goes into the world in search of moments that prick him or her. These are moments which puncture, and here, I'm drawing from Barthes' *Camera Lucida* where he addresses the distinction between *studium* and *punctum*. The *studium*, he writes, is "that very wide field of unconcerned desire, of various interest, of inconsequential taste" while the *punctum* is "that accident which pricks me" (*Camera Lucida* 27). While Barthes was writing about the reading of a photograph, here, I am applying the terms to the practice of street photography. The *studium* is the field of actions surrounding the photographer, while *punctum* is that which "pricks" him or her in a way that may not be immediately comprehended. I do not mean that the street photographer is that sensitive soul who is somehow able to "capture" meaningful scenes in the flux of experience. What I do mean is that the photographer is able to figure out that certain scenes might be more fruitful for the retrospective work of thinking, looking and reading.

For example, this

This is a primordial scene for me. I am on a double-decker bus in a tunnel. This is a tunnel vision of sorts, acknowledging that how anything we choose to look at or talk about is always partial. Yet the focus is on the passengers, on other people, even though it is impossible for the street photographer to be completely outside the frame of his own photograph. We are all in the end on the same journey, emerging from this birth tunnel to our different destinations. This idea, provoked by the photograph, is the work of street photography.

The documentary and the poetic are perhaps the two most important desires for someone who is interested in the aesthetics. It is the documentary desire that allows us to take a "top down approach" to the reading of a work. Once we recognize something as modernist, for example, we automatically surround the work within a particular ecology of ideas and concepts. The poetic desire, however, involves entering into a work and experiencing the flow of ideas, impulses and sometimes the shock of the new. This venture into street photography allows me to extend, and as a result, articulate some of the tensions I work with as a professional academic. We tend to highlight the textual at the expense of the social and personal. I think I have given in too much to the documentary desire, relying on social categories rather than lived experience. In other words, I talk like a sociologist examining a text, rather than as a writer about some of the struggles a writer would face. I feel as if I am reaching too easily for concepts. For the academic, the death-of-the-author thesis and the author-function argument have become a totalitarian force.

What does the artist or poet or street photographer know that sets him or her apart from the professionalized academic? Perhaps they know what it means to struggle towards a solution to the question their art puts to them. This is what I am getting at with the phrase "poetic desire". As James Elkins puts it: "There's a tidal pull, in art discourse, away from kinds of knowledge that can be argued propositionally, and toward things that cannot be logically clarified, but that can somehow still be called knowledge" (*What Do Artists Know?* 45). Poetic desire, too, is a kind of knowledge.

What, then, can be passed on by showing you the next photograph and poem?:

how hong kong works

how hong kong works, no one knows,
though everyone says *mm goi*, *mm goi*,
thank you, small favour, another name
for waiter, excuse me, help.

it's excessive when one says *mm goi sai*
at a pedestrian crossing – we simply turn and go.

how at the end of the day it's the numbers
that meet, a shiny car going too fast,
the bottom line, a business suit,
a kind of bright easy love making
sense between tony leung and maggie cheung.

tony leung and maggie cheung,
we ready our mouths for the vowels,
those easy rhymes between money,
cha chaan teng, fame, a coach handbag,
happiness in a teacup.

hi in Cantonese is a vulgarity,
lei ho a politeness among colleagues,
ni hao these days is an estate agent greeting
a mainland buyer.

wai over the phone
pre-empts that unsolicited sales call.

(why, why do you call me.)

how hong kong works, no one knows,
though everyone says *mm goi*, *mm goi*,
thank you, small favour, another name
for waiter, excuse me, help.

it's excessive when one says mm goi sai
at a pedestrian crossing – we simply turn and go.

how at the end of the day
we all wait to enter a building –
the locked door to the corner office opens
and we will hear well done, come in,
good good, *thank you*, *hello*, *goodbye*.

(Tay, *Dreaming Cities*, 3-5)

Like the previous photograph, this was taken on board a double-decker bus. You can see that the subject was sitting across from me, and the contemplative posture and somewhat grungy hairstyle spoke to me. That the bus went past Chungking Mansions a few seconds before I pulled out my camera was significant. It is a Wong Kar-wai *Chungking Express* moment for me, in that there is an artlessly gritty aesthetic at work which speaks of Hong Kong's existential condition in the period of late capitalism. Hong Kong is representative of a kind of late modernity that is immersed in a hyper-abundance of signs and cultural meanings in a state of flux. There is a sense that something of socio-political significance is always happening, and there are various street protests and demonstrators with various agendas, all of it to do with a kind of hyper-capitalism existing hand-in-hand with political disenfranchisement, with no resolution in sight. That is a self-portrait of sorts, a kind of Nirvana-in-Carnegie-Hall aesthetic. I am gesturing towards a kind of inchoate felt-experience of urban spaces.

I am going to invoke the very loaded term "negative capability" which Keats elaborates as being "capable of being in uncertainties, Mysteries, doubts, without any irritable reaching after fact & reason" (Keats 193). I evoke this term to indicate a state of mind that remains open to various possibilities, that is suspicious of packaged experiences, sedimented ideas, and set ways of doing things. Negative capability is that stick which stirs the sediments beneath the water, mucking up things and disrupting settled ways of thought.

negative capability

today i shall be a clueless tourist
in my own country of the self:

i tell my son i am a tree
though I am a tree trying to be a man

because it takes ten years to cultivate a tree,
a century for a human being;

sometimes i have to be a rock
though I am a rock trying to be a man

because jesus was a rock,
and peter was a rock;

on other days i tell my boss
i am a calculator

though i am a calculator trying to be a man
because a calculator is convenient;

am i a pencil that i must write,
or am i to be water?

i tell myself i am a camera
though i am a camera trying to be a man

because a camera captures everything
and is nothing in itself.

(Tay, *Dreaming Cities*, 84-85)

I have come to think of photography, as well as poetry, as visual and verbal search engines of modern life. In a way, I am searching for an image of myself.

Is it possible for a camera to be regarded as a tool for preserving one's autonomy? Time and again, I come back to this series of images taken in Singapore:

Public housing in Singapore is managed by the Housing and Development Board (HDB), a statutory board of the Ministry of National Development. Singaporean citizens could purchase these new and subsidized flats directly from the government provided they meet various criteria. The housing policies are generally pro-family, pro-marriage and heteronormative. Given that about 80-85% of Singaporeans live in public housing, you can see, then, how Singapore reinforces its middle-class, pro-capitalist and multicultural ethos on its populace. Public housing is in many ways an ideological state apparatus. In films such as Eric Khoo's *12 Storeys*, and Jack Neo's *Money No Enough* and *I Not Stupid*, HDB flats are symbols of middle-class, cookie-cutter culture.

It is easy to portray public housing in such a way, but I want to suggest that there is a potential for transformation and newness as well out of a homogenous and typified existence:

A tree could explode against the facade of a HDB flat, signifying life, disruption and change. Public housing, and by extension, most urban spaces are functions of organized and rational thought that slots people into heteronormative and stratified social classifications. We are always interpellated as consumers, committed citizens, and workers. I am also reminded of Simmel's point that

> [t]he deepest problems of modern life derive from the claim of the individual to preserve the autonomy and individuality of his existence in the face of overwhelming social forces, …of external culture, and of the technique of life. (Simmel 409)

The act of writing poetry and the practice of street photography is such that the urban space can also be a background for another way of looking, thinking, and acting. How may we look, act and think otherwise?

I wish to highlight the following passage by James Elkins:

> Every field of vision is clotted with sexuality, desire, convention, anxiety, and boredom, and nothing is available for full, leisurely inspection. Seeing is also inconstant seeing, partial seeing, poor seeing, and not seeing, or to put it as strongly as possible…seeing involves and entails blindness; seeing is also blindness. (Elkins *The Object Stares Back* 95)

I want to be able to see my blindness, or to know there are things I am looking at but do not see. Is the following photograph about commodity fetishism, about the power of brands in conferring and confirming one's station in life? Or is it about a gaze that is appropriative, in which street photography seeks its vengeance on advertising photography, subjecting its persuasive power to critique? Advertising photography is a work of art, in as much as the viewing of advertising photography is also a work of critique. Again, I seek to be poetic, not documentary. This is not a document that testifies to the power of commodity, but (I hope) a poetic rendering of another way of seeing.

The point has been made by many people, including Susan Sontag, that the street photographer is a *flâneur* of sorts. Sontag has many criticisms about photography in her book *On Photography*. As she puts it,

> A way of certifying experience, taking photographs is also a way of refusing it – by limiting experience to a search for the photogenic, by converting experience into an image, a souvenir. (Sontag 9)

I am thinking of people I know who like to photograph their food before they eat, or of parents who take photographs of their children while they are playing the piano at home or of their families in front of the Eiffel Tower. There is nothing wrong with doing these things (I do them myself all the time). But after a while, if we claim to be serious about photography as an art form and yet this is all we do with photography, then it no longer allows us to see anything new. It allows us to see only what we already see, putting us in a state of self-consuming and self-affirming narcissism, saying, "Look at me, look at me".

Sontag's views are thought-provoking:

> Photography implies that we know about the world if we accept it as the camera records it. But this is the opposite of understanding, which starts from *not* accepting the world as it looks. [italics in original] (23)

What if we pursue photography with humility, as a way of looking at things differently? John Berger has made the point that "Every photograph presents us with two messages: a message concerning the event photographed and another concerning the shock of discontinuity" (*Another Way of Telling* 86). He goes on to say that "Between the moment recorded and the present moment of looking at the photograph, there is an abyss" (*Another Way of Telling* 87). While Sontag focuses on the moment of taking the photograph, Berger gets us thinking about the act of looking at a photograph. This abyss then, is what we are in right now and what we have been trying to cope with. The abyss is when the street photograph gives us something we find hard to accept. We look, and look again, and we struggle with the meaning of the scene.

Here, then, is the condition of street photography. It aspires to the condition of found poetry in its search for the readymade scene. It is not the street scene that waits for the arrival of the photographer, but the photographer who designates the street as such. Can one be persuaded that the scene in the above photograph is an everyday scene?

The photographic subject above is a tantalizing figure. One peruses the newspapers over breakfast at home or at a *cha chaan teng*. The newspaper reader, utterly at ease and reposed on an office chair on a street pavement, is declaring that he owns the streets. He refuses to obey the unspoken rules concerning public and private space, concerning what is or is not done on the streets of Hong Kong. Has anyone said it is wrong to be at ease, reading a newspaper like this in an office chair on a street pavement? The street photographer aspires to this pose of reading at leisure.

I am reminded also of Benedict Anderson's point concerning the relationship between the act of reading a newspaper and one's national consciousness. Anderson describes the act of reading a newspaper as a "mass ceremony":

> [the newspaper reader is] well aware that the ceremony he performs is being replicated simultaneously by thousands (or millions) of others of whose existence he is confident, yet of whose identity he has not the slightest notion. (35)

As Anderson asks, "What more vivid figure for the secular, historically clocked, imagined community can be envisioned?" (35). One could project one's hopes onto the photographic subject – it represents the consciousness of an imagined community laying claim to the public as well as the psycho-geographical spaces of Hong Kong. Anderson's notion of the imagined community is something we will return to time and again in this book.

I hope by now I have conveyed a sense of what the linked practices of poetry, street photography and scholarship are about – they are about reading, looking and thinking with poetic desire, they are about searching for that moment when one is pricked by a scene, a scene in which everyday life transformed into poetry. They are also, for me personally, a way of reconciling the practice of street photography and writing poetry with scholarship. As Max van Manen puts it,

> Not unlike the poet, the phenomenologist directs the gaze toward the regions where meaning originates, wells up, percolates through the porous membranes of past sedimentations—and then infuses us, permeates us, infects us, touches us, stirs us, exercises a formative affect. (12)

I am trying, in the end, to work on a kind of research that attends to the phenomenology of practice, a kind of scholarship that I can get away with:

end of tunnel

i am tired of metaphors with ants
crawling like an efficient army above
and to the side of a head
of branch felled from a tree

i realise i have to learn
to write another way
perhaps with a spear of light

writing with light
so i could crawl
out of a private tunnel
of a vision

with some practice
the roof of the tunnel
becomes the ceiling of my mouth
and the ground the floor of my tongue
the walls the inside of my cheeks

only then will i be a spit
of myself walking away
free at last from the tunnel
from words drifting like dead leaves

(Tay, *Dreaming Cities*, 58-59)

TOWARDS A WRITING PRACTICE

I read, think and look with poetic desire. I am trying to get away with a desire that cannot be separated from Hong Kong and Singapore, the two cities I call home. I write critically and creatively about, in and despite the cities of Hong Kong and Singapore. I write with and against the grain of these two frenetic cities that privilege a capitalist-oriented mentality at the expense of a contemplative writing life. What is creative writing for Hong Kong and Singapore, and what are Hong Kong and Singapore for creative writing? Creative writing, Hong Kong, Singapore…there is the problem of proper names, proper nouns, proper concepts…how may we render these names, nouns and concepts into a flow of meaning and channel them into an interiority, into the scene and mental life of writing? Drawing from the lessons of autoethnography and phenomenology, I am in search of a language that describes a specific practice of creative writing, a language that explores the notions of superficiality, mythification and irreality, for these are conditions situated within the particularities of my experience as a creative writer in Hong Kong and Singapore.

So I begin with Hélène Cixious: "What is most true is poetic. What is most true is naked life. I can only attain this mode of seeing with the aid of poetic writing. I apply myself to 'seeing' the world nude…with the naked, obstinate, defenceless eye of my nearsightedness" (Cixous and Calle-Gruber 3). I am trying to write without the use of prostheses, even as I acknowledge that this is an impossible situation. To write is to submit to multiple levels of disciplines, from the keyboard to the word processing software, located within an office embedded within the institutional parameters of a university, and I am addressing my peers in other universities, other institutions, other writing locations, who are social actors like myself, embedded within this imaginary academic-disciplinary field of creative writing studies. To write is to submit to the apparatus of a discipline. To write is to be a social agent caught within contingencies of writing. I cannot write naked, but I can write with compromises, and these days, to be compromised is to be true.

I am inspired by the above quotation from Cixious and by a particular passage we have seen previously in Simmel's essay "The Metropolis and Mental Life", where he argues that individuals need to protect their "autonomy and individuality" against "external culture, and…the technique of life" (Simmel *Sociology* 409). Both passages are significant in terms of articulating the central concern here. While Cixous writes powerfully from an overflowing interiority, Simmel reminds us of externalities that exert pressure on how we write. As such, I am interested in mapping an interiority to creative writing that at the same time is aware of its immersed condition within the exterior social and cultural environments of Hong Kong and Singapore. Hence, I see myself as exploring the grounds of exteriority and interiority that make possible the practice of creative writing. I write towards a socio-philosophy of creative writing, paying attention to the social environments of Hong Kong and Singapore; at the same time, I think upon how external social and urban pressures create an interiority for the writer and perhaps, *vice versa*.

I am interested in mapping an interiority in so far as it could be mapped by writing. There is the argument that writing is way of life, a way of life that escapes the physical confines of the page even as it motivates the physical act of writing. How is one to live in order to write? How is one to write in order to live? Perhaps they are the same questions. Time and again I am tempted by the possibilities of expressing a singularity, a coherence, even as I am sometimes torn between various kinds of languages. A critical language acceptable to academia, an unruly language that produces poetry, a range of personal languages heard only by my intimate loved ones, a range of socially acceptable collegial language I exchange frequently with friends, colleagues and acquaintances. A language I reserve for myself. A language in which I reserve myself.

And I find myself having to explain myself to myself, reminding myself of the subtitle to Friedrich Nietzsche's *Ecce Homo*, "How One Becomes What One is". What is one but many? I refuse to reduce my self (selves) to the constraints of a single language. I avail myself of a delinquency, sometimes writing the way one is not supposed to write, sometimes writing the way one is supposed to write. I cannot regard language as an unproblematic medium. I am suspicious of it. I use it because I have no choice. Language is a problem. If we allow language its invisibility, we risk losing Other(s) within ourselves that are struggling to emerge. This is how I conceive the project of becoming who I am. Alexander Nehamas explains Nietzsche's doctrine as follows: "To be who one is…is to be engaged in a constantly continuing and continually broadening process of appropriation of one's experiences and actions" (Nehamas 190-191). This paradoxical injunction articulates the challenge of thinking about writing. How is one to become who one is as a writer? If a self is comprised at least of a series of experiential or mental episodes, then I offer the following two for consideration.

—

Episode one: I am thinking of a literary prize winner. She was one of the English Category winners of the Golden Point Award 2009. I remember watching her read her poem at The Arts House, Singapore's former Parliament House that has been converted into an arts venue, during the Singapore Writers Festival

2009. And I remember seeing her a few hours later after the reading, walking towards a bus stop. I remember thinking this poet is now no longer a poet but an undifferentiated, anonymous, member of a Singaporean public in the cityscape. I remember it was mentioned that she worked for the Ministry of Education. When is one a writer and when is one not a writer? I have returned to this moment many times because of what it entails. The technique of modern living compels one to live multiple roles, to attend to the business of making a living, to drive those half-articulated motivations and impulses underground even as one leads an outwardly productive life.

Even as these impulses emerge in the form of poetry or fiction, as literary forms they are subject to categorization, institutionalization, role-playing. The Golden Point Award is organized by Singapore's National Arts Council and it is a biennial literary competition for unpublished works in English, Chinese, Malay and Tamil which are the four official languages of Singapore. Her poem had won a prize in the English Category of the Golden Point Award, and hence entered into culture through bureaucratization of a prize aligned with the multiculturalist policy of the nation state of Singapore.

Episode two: I had accepted an invitation to be part of two panel discussions at the Hong Kong International Literary Festival 2012. Even as I am honored to have been invited, I am not completely at ease with some of the topics to be discussed. We are to discuss avenues for creative writing publication and related activities, as well as the role of English language writers in Hong Kong and Asia. Creative writing is socialized, disciplined, professionalized and projected onto a public. We have yet to learn to speak a language that attends to the unthought in writing. Apart from being able to say that writing involves the act of immersing oneself in an experience of which an outcome has yet to be fully determined at the beginning, what else could one say? Would that which is potentially radical in writing be neutralized as a result of the writer being cast as occupying a useful and accepted role in society? Is there space for the unthought in the social sphere as well as within the creative writing industry, a way of thinking, writing and teaching differently?

These two episodes articulate what is at stake in creative writing studies as an academic and professionalized field, as well as creative writing as texts and performances in the social arena. How is the writer to perform in public and at the same time, reserve space for the unthought to enter the world? I am interested in a language that understands the necessity of its being voided of sociality, at the same time, however, it is to be a language utterable by someone inhabiting a social function. A language that is not wholly social is madness. Here, I am reminded of Foucault's comments: "Madness appears as an utterance wrapped up in itself, articulating something else beneath what it says, of which it is at the same time the only possible code" ("Madness" 295). Madness, in other words, is self-consuming; it is a language that has folded into itself. How do we usher the unthought into the social sphere? Hence, I am offering the following terms, namely, superficiality, mythification and irreality; terms which refer to conditions within which we must work in order for writing to avoid its madness, for it to be productive and transformative in this social sphere.

EMBRACING SUPERFICIALITY: FINDING A PLACE

How does one find a place for creative writing in such hyper-capitalist cities as Hong Kong and Singapore? The grand narratives of both Hong Kong and Singapore may be described in terms of a transition from colonial to global capitalism. Obviously, there are important differences to the social, cultural, political and economic landscapes of the two cities, but suffice to say, one cannot but be confronted by the capitalist-oriented nature of Hong Kong and Singapore when thinking and living in these two cities. Even as the writer knows that the capitalist system is beyond the influence of any single individual, he or she is located within it and immersed in its particularities. Is creative writing an escape (however fantasized a form that escape may take) or is it constitutive of capitalism?

David Fenza has argued that the creative writing program is a space where the writer could escape from what he sees as mindless and rampant consumerism that pervades everyday life (211). However, it may be argued that a writer is not going to be in a creative writing program forever. He or she has to forge his or her own relations with the world. Furthermore, if the role of the writer is to somehow draw his material from his everyday life, then he or she has to come to terms with the totality which is capitalism in which he or she is immersed. Sooner or later, someone is going to come along to inspect the goods. As Fenza himself has argued, even as we locate the sphere of creative writing "free from the pressures of the marketplace", we nonetheless hope that our writings become a viable product in the very same marketplace (209).

Perhaps capitalism is the writer's saving grace in that it provides a ready-made solution, an alibi, if you will, to the examined life. It might be useful to turn to crude monetary valuation as a way of forestalling the existential abyss which confronts the modern artist:

> For the deeper person there is only one possibility of enduring life
> at all: a certain measure of superficiality. For if he were to ponder
> all the conflicting, irreconcilable impulses, duties, strivings, and
> yearnings as deeply, to feel them all as absolutely and ultimately
> as their nature and his properly require – then he would have to
> explode, go crazy, or run out on life. (Simmel *View of Life* 168)

What, then, is the market for the artist? What is capitalism for the creative writer? One should *escape into* the market, into means-ends valuation, into the rational calculation of the value of one's work. Superficiality is the sign of a mature artist so long as it allows for sustainable creative work. I agree with Fenza that one should posit the creative writing program as a solution to capitalism. But while Fenza conceives of creative writing program as a refuge from capitalism and its attendant consumerist-oriented values, I would say that the creative writing program is constitutive of capitalism itself, itself a source of tuition dollars for colleges and universities. One thinks, of course, of the job market for creative writers, of creative writers who hold teaching appointments in academia; there is much about teaching and a literary education that is valuable in itself, of course, but the creative writer, by attending to the means-ends calculation, would find a place for himself or herself so as to pursue his or her art. Of course, what is happening here is the commodification of the writer and his or her work. Therefore I am in agreement with Fenza in an ironic manner. For Fenza, the creative writing program is a refuge from mindless consumerism; for me the creative writing program (and by extension, the academia) is a useful *escape into* mindless means-ends calculation so as to follow Simmel's advice, which is to endure life via "a certain measure of superficiality" (Simmel 2010, 168). At the very least, superficiality could be put to good use: the credentials afforded by the academic institutions could be used to further one's art. We really need to be honest about the economic situation of creative writers teaching in the university: even as we possess an aura of freedom and autonomy in our work, our work is economically sustainable because we have found a place to operate within the ambit of the division of intellectual labor.

Writers from Hong Kong and Singapore have varied professional backgrounds. In other words, they are not all full time writers. A lot of them have truly high profile careers as lawyers and bankers. A novelist and poet I have in mind is a specialist lawyer in corporate mergers and acquisitions, another is a quant – he is a risk analyst dealing with complicated financial statistics in an international bank. Hence, what I am getting at is that there is no line to be drawn between the space of creative writing and the space of capitalism. The means-ends thinking as well as the vocabulary of capitalism has been put to good use, I would think, in order to foster the act of creative writing. Strategies that pertain to professional networking, events promotion, digital presence, and so on, have been put to good use. If such things are superficial, then I would think we need to take superficiality seriously so as to make profound the mental life of the creative writer. As a writer, one must pay heed to the intensity of one's emotions, observations, and experimentations with language as a solitary being with the privilege of writing in a room of one's own, and at the same time, be aware that that room is made possible because it is part of a larger social, cultural and capitalist regime. The collusion between the superficial and the profound in creative writing has already been signaled by Virginia Woolf when she wrote of the material realities of the writer and her environment. Of course, she was talking about the female writer, but I am interested in adapting her question to make it applicable to the creative writer in Hong Kong and Singapore – how is the writer to find a mental room of his or her own in the hyper-capitalist cities of Hong Kong and Singapore? I bring this up not because I am offering a solution here – there are no solutions. But I believe this is one of the questions a creative writer has to live with every day: how superficial must one be so as to be able to pursue one's art with profundity?

MYTHIFICATION: THE IRONIC SITUATION OF THE WRITER

Creative writing is an activity, a way of life within a social sphere which compels one to enact certain roles which "makes sense" to a public. The question of the practice of creative writing is partly a question of the construction of a self for others. The creative writer is a social agent in a creative writing industry, immersed in capitalistic ventures partly to advertise and sell his or her writing. (In the case of the creative writer located within academia, he or she of course, sells her skills as a teacher.) There is of course a limit to that superficiality in that one needs to be aware of the possible mythification of one's vocation. I am using here Roland Barthes' notion of myth. As he puts it, "'Bourgeois', 'petit-bourgeois', 'capitalism', 'proletariat' are the locus of an unceasing haemorrhage: meaning flows out of them until their very name becomes unnecessary" (Barthes 1972, 138). Myths, for Barthes, refer to how the ideological system (in this case, capitalism and its attendant values such as individualism, meritocracy and democracy) that governs society creates "truths" out of social and everyday phenomena.

When one uses words like "lyrical power", "truth" and "beauty", one really has to consider the entanglement of these terms with the aura of freedom and autonomy of the writer. Creative writing is a form of social praxis in that the realm of the arts has become the repository of the lack which characterizes means-ends thinking of business people, bureaucrats and those who work in the various professions. If the rules governing businesses and the management of institutions are often impersonal, then art is personal. If the for-profit motive often leads to brutal consequences, then art has to be lyrical. If it is deemed correct for one to adopt a professional façade when dealing with people, then art has to be authentic and true. In their essay "The Culture Industry: Enlightenment as Mass Deception", Max Horkheimer and Theodor W. Adorno make the point that "[t]he triumph of advertising in the culture industry is that consumers feel compelled to buy and use its products even though they see through them" (167). One could say the same for the culture industry of creative writing: we as creative writers feel compelled to use the language of autonomy even though we see through them.

In her book *Creativity and Its Discontents*, Laikwan Pang has made the point that the creative industry approaches the notion of creativity in a contradictory manner. She writes that "creativity is not only democratized but also fetishized by our education system and popular culture" such that it becomes both an "elitist and democratic" ideal (62). On the one hand, we celebrate creative individuals such as Steve Jobs – we believe his influence and success is a result of his inherent creative personality. On the other hand, creativity is supposedly accessible to anyone, provided he or she has the right tools, be it the latest IPad, IPhone and the latest app. One might say the same of the creative writer in the classroom, in that even as we attribute profundity and depth of thought and emotions to the creative writer (terms that, embarrassingly, are often applied to myself), we would like to believe that these attributes are accessible to the ordinary person – if only he or she would enroll in our creative writing classes.

On the one hand, we do believe in creativity in so far as there is an implicit promise of transcendence; we value the act of trying to go beyond oneself and looking beyond one's material circumstance, immersing oneself in the aesthetic experience. On the other hand, an overvaluing of creativity lends itself easily to the reified professional language of the culture industry. There is also the argument that a training in creative writing prepares graduates to work in a range of industries where good writing is crucial, including cultural and arts administration, as well as in the areas of editing, publishing and social media marketing.

How may we go beyond this impasse? Perhaps the stance of the writer has to be an ironic one. On the one hand, we are immersed in superficiality, and we are sustained on myths; on the other hand, we hope to be able to redeem ourselves through the possibility of transcendence, a form of thinking beyond the self that is promised through the work of creative writing. Perhaps we have to learn to recognize the irony of our situation in that even as the practice of creative writing is surrounded by an aura of freedom and autonomy (we think we have chosen the path of writing), in actual fact, given our dispositions, temperament and orientations – it is not that we choose to write, but that writing chooses us and we must follow.

Jean-Paul Sartre's notion of irreality is useful when thinking about how poets seek to convert the nouns of their cities into the flow of their writing. In *The Imaginary*, Sartre embarks on a phenomenological investigation of the imagination. The final portions of his book are especially interesting in that he posits that works of art present irreality. In the act of reading poems, viewing paintings, or listening to music, we read, view and listen within the space of the imaginary (Sartre *Imaginary* 193). There is on the one hand the material and concrete qualities of the works of art that we perceive. On the other hand, we apprehend these within the imaginary such that they are given a wholeness that is not possible in the act of perception. Sartre explains this using the example of a cube. Our visual perception is such that we cannot see all six sides of a cube at the same time (Sartre *Imaginary* 8). Nonetheless the six sides are present in our total imaginary apprehension of the very same cube. The imaginary six-sided cube is hence irreal (but no less true) in relation to the real cube we see before us.

What is creative writing for Hong Kong and Singapore, and what are Hong Kong and Singapore for creative writing? Creative writing, Hong Kong, Singapore…there is the problem of proper names, proper nouns, proper concepts…how may we render these names, nouns and concepts into a flow of meaning and channel them into an interiority, into the scene and mental life of writing? We may then begin to answer this question. Even as the creative writer is immersed in superficiality, even as he or she is struggling with mythification of his or her work, because the nature of the work lies in the irreal, there is then the freedom to go beyond proper nouns. As in the example of the cube, we cannot see all of Hong Kong or all of Singapore. But in the imaginary we could allow emanations of Hong Kong or Singapore to emerge. I am gesturing towards what Sartre calls the "poetic attitude" regarding language, in that words are things in themselves and not signs pointing to something external to the words (Sartre *What is Literature?* 12).

What happens when we pay attention to this poetic attitude when reading poems about Singapore and Hong Kong? Toh Hsien Min, a Singaporean poet who read literature at Oxford, is a certified financial accountant whose day job as a quantitative risk analyst in an international bank requires him to negotiate between means-ends thinking of high finance with the call of a poetic work that opens us to the realm of an imaginary Singapore. It is no surprise that his poetry collection is entitled *Means to an End*. Some of his poems, such as the wonderfully titled "The Happiness of Meaning in the New Economy" and "HR in the Time of Recession", beautifully capture the *ennui* of professionals in the superficially successful, modern Singapore. A number of his poems are always situated at the beginning of the imaginary scene. His poem "The Bridges" draws attention to the beginning of the imagination at the scene of coming to terms with one's sense of self: "we imagine we want to / remember more than we can remember, or want to" (Toh *Means* 9). At the same time, as his poem "Birth of the Modern City-State" tells us, the sense of self of its inhabitants is circumscribed by the official, impersonal site which is the city of Singapore:

> We only remember because
> there was something in each of these streetlamps of memory
> to fix them beside those double yellow lines. There was
> only something because of the architecture of the city
> to which we all subscribe, and which still shapes and
> outlines what we are for as long as we are it. (Toh *Means* 13)

The phrase "streetlamps of memory" echoes the streetlamps we find in T. S. Eliot's "Preludes" and "Rhapsody on a Windy Night". Eliot's poems represent existential withdrawals into the wrecked self of the modern European man. In contrast, Toh's poems hint at a positivity, a building up of a self. It is a poem that accuses Singapore of clinging on to its official and touristic symbols such as the Merlion and the Cenotaph at the expense of forging an interior attunement to the city:

> Now that we are here, now that to the left you see
> the stage-managing, perspectivally mobile chrysalides
> and the pier making the newly perched Merlion
> photographable from the sea, we must remember to turn
> right to the Cenotaph and the Tan Kim Seng fountain. (Toh *Means* 12)

While the poem is conscious of the constraints and regulations, "those double yellow lines" of the city-state of Singapore, it is nonetheless able to dwell on and look to the beyond of the official city-state. The city "outlines what we are for as long as we are it" (Toh *Means* 13)". The point is not to be it. The poem warns us against the prosaic attitude towards the city, an attitude which allows externalities to shape one's inner life. We refuse to be it. We refuse the external forces of the city but instead allow it to enter the imaginary so as to turn it into an object. It is in the poem that the writer resists and reshapes the city, as demonstrated by the poems of Madeleine Slavick.

Slavick has lived in Hong Kong for close to two decades. Her poems constantly draw attention to the city as a poetic composition. In the poem "city automatic", all objects in the city are poetic material:

Unseen machines buzz   trucks carry   lift   and throw trash like
tired football stars
                    crosswalks blink   at each other
                    buses lunge
can I take away one sound? (Slavick 16)

There is an intentionality that overrides this irreal city of Hong Kong. In her poem
"subway searching", for example, the gaze of the poet-persona in the subway
cabin is a disturbing one, often moving from one expressionless and impersonal
face to another. Nonetheless:

the search wants to end with a fifty-year-old hand living
on a woman's thigh   let us count their loved years (Slavick 18)

It is no coincidence that her poetry collection is titled *delicate access*, drawing
attention to the care with which one might enter the irreality of Hong Kong:

and let us count the dust on a construction man's surrendered
shoulders, on his mouth open in shock, his red eyes, blacker
eyelashes: he is dying, dying tonight, while the Wednesday
horses cover his newsprint with prayer and fate
                              win, this moment, win (Slavick 18)

Slavick is drawing attention to the futility of wanting more for Hong Kong. The
searching gaze wants to end in an act of affection, it wants to count the dust on a
man's shoulders, it wants to win for itself a moment that is meaningful.

The poems of Toh and Slavick are arrested in the act of transcendence, moving
from the real city to the irreal city, with the hope of emerging back into the
real with meaning, validity, and attainment. Both poets write with the hope that
the intentionalities articulated in the poems will overflow from the writing and
spill into the social materiality of the real. As Sartre puts it, "words are there like
traps to arouse our feelings and to reflect them toward us. Each word is a path of
transcendence" (*What is Literature?* 45). Both Toh and Slavick are poets who are
sensitive to the cities in which they live. It is as if to say that the world around
them flows into their texts, and the poems signal their indexicality even as they
articulate various intentionalities. In the case of Toh, this intentionality warns us
of the dangers of being narrowly defined by the official circumscriptions of the
city in which one lives. In Slavick's case, we are given a moment of affection
in a public, impersonal space. The poems are doing the work of ushering the
unthought into emergence.

Nehamas, in his reading of Nietzsche's work, writes of the quest to rediscover and re-invent one's values: "Our creations eventually become our truths, and our truths circumscribe our creations" (174). Superficiality, mythification, irreality – these are the truths of the conditions of writing. It remains for me to say that these are truths that are built up and situated within the particularities of my experience as a creative writer, and hence represent an engagement with a number of issues that are grounded experientially that may be relevant to others. I offer these thoughts not as realities to be validated, but rather in the spirit of searching for affinity with fellow creative writers who I imagine to be like me, searching for a language to describe what it is that we do.

MULTICULTURALISMS, MISTRANSLATIONS AND BILINGUAL POETRY

Even as we write to rediscover and reinvent our values, the writing self, as well as the practice of creative writing and translation, is subject to cultural, political, linguistic and institutional influences. As a creative writer who flirts with translation (or mistranslation) rather than a scholar of translation studies, I am very much intrigued by the poet-translator's role "as a 'reader-creator' and as 'self-writer'" (Perteghella 2).

My first home language is Hokkien, the language spoken in Taiwan as well as in the Fujian province of China. In contrast, within Singapore's education curriculum, the medium of instruction is English. In addition to English, students take classes in their Mother Tongues (Mandarin for the Chinese, Malay for the Malays and Tamil for the Indians). It has been noted by many that the term "Mother Tongue" is problematic, for Tamil and Mandarin are in most cases not the respective home languages for the Indian and Chinese communities in Singapore. So what really happens to my Chinese friends and myself is that our first home languages (be it Hokkien, Cantonese, Hakka, Teochew and so on) is put aside, to be replaced by English, the language of instruction in school, as well as Mandarin.

Our language proficiencies are influenced by Singapore's bilingual education policy, which is a function of what is known as the CMIO (Chinese, Malay, Indian, Others) multiculturalist policy. I am using the term "multiculturalism" here in the way Ien Ang uses it, to denote "a government policy [that] manage[s] cultural diversity within a pluralist nation-state" (14). Multiculturalism, Ang argues, "depends on the fixing of mutually exclusive identities" (14). In the case of Singapore, the ethnic classification of CMIO has the effect of reifying ethnic group identities, and in the process rendering invisible the multilingual nature of each ethnic group. L. Quentin Dixon has argued that Singapore's education policy "succeeded in shifting home language use from Chinese dialects to Mandarin and, perhaps unintentionally, from vernaculars and official Mother Tongues to English" (42). He stresses that "[w]hen this [bilingual] policy was implemented, virtually no one spoke English or Mandarin as their home language and only a small elite reached high levels of English or Mandarin proficiency" (42-43).

What this means is that Singapore's contemporary linguistic landscape is a result of successful social engineering on the part of the state. Each ethnic community has its own official Mother Tongue, as well as English. While each Mother Tongue supposedly represents the cultural repository of each of the three main ethnic community, the English language is normalized by Singapore's nation building discourse as "neutral and cultureless", to be used "for instrumental and pragmatic reasons" (Rubdy 342). It is considered the global language and hence, a medium through which Singaporeans remain connected to the world. At the same time, it is used for "inter-ethnic communication" within Singapore (Rubdy 344). However, when we look at recent developments in Singapore literature, it is Anglophone poetry and fiction that form the bulk of writings. The emergence of Anglophone literature in Singapore is testimony to the fact that English is more than just a "neutral" and "cultureless" language. Robbie B. H. Goh has pointed out that many of the writers who have emerged in the recent two decades were "product[s] of the post-independence social policies that have created a largely monolingual, well-educated and cosmopolitan Anglophone elite" ("Anxiety of Influences" 48).

Nonetheless, there is a tendency for the CMIO system to be replicated in literary production. The term "boutique multiculturalism" has been applied to the literature of Singapore. Tamara S. Wagner has drawn attention to "the enormous marketability of consciously 'exotic' representations" at work (32). She draws the term from Stanley Fish, who defines boutique multiculturalism as "the multiculturalism of ethnic restaurants [and] weekend festivals" (378). For Fish, "Boutique multiculturalism is characterized by its superficial or cosmetic relationship to the objects of its affection" (378). He argues that "a boutique multiculturalist does not and cannot take seriously the core values of the cultures he tolerates" (Fish 379). In order to preserve a semblance of multicultural harmony, lines are drawn, marking out one cultural sphere from another. What this means is that there is a line the cultural Other cannot cross, for if it does, it will be regarded as a transgression of the social order.

While there is very little visible ethnic segregation within the social sphere, the same cannot be said of the cultural sphere. In Singapore, the prestigious Golden Point Award which is a national literary competition organized by the National Arts Council gives out first, second and third prizes in each of the English, Chinese, Malay and Tamil sections. A poem written in English, for instance, may not compete with one written in Malay. The works of prize winners are published in the form of booklets, complete with English translations. Likewise, the title of Edwin Thumboo's 1990 poetry anthology *Words for the 25th* betrays the nationalist agenda of the collection, 1990 being the 25th anniversary of the independence of Singapore. Again, there are four sections to the collection, consisting of translations of Malay, Tamil, Chinese poetry as well as an "English Section". On the one hand, one may say that such a strategy allows for the work of each ethnic group to be represented. On the other hand, boutique multiculturalism as reflected in this collection is characterized by separation of reified ethnic essences, calling to mind Ang's statement that "multiculturalism is based on the fantasy that the social challenge of togetherness-in-difference can be addressed by reducing it to an image of living-apart-together" (14). In these publications, no space is given to the translators' commentary. Hence, the invisibility of the work of translators which maintains the hierarchy between the original and translation becomes complicit in keeping the cultural work of ethnic groups in their separate ethnic spheres under the guise of promoting ethnic representation.

The CMIO system certainly allows for ethnic representation in a country composed of various ethnic groups. Yet the problem with the system is that it reifies the self-identical nature of ethnicity. The assumption is that just because one is Chinese, one supposedly possesses some kind of immanent Chinese cultural knowledge. The following is a stanza taken from the poem "three love objects" by Teng Qian Xi, who writes against this assumption of immanent Chinese cultural knowledge. Her poem unveils the gap between the poet and her Chinese cultural inheritance:

> Li Shangyin (813–858) lights his candle.
> *The night sighs at the chill of moonlight.*
> Longing flakes across his desk.
> *The wax dries into ash and the tears are dry.*
> He writes a scorched-earth policy.
> *Incense smoke passes through the gold lock.*
> Torch what you want and can't take with you.
> *For each inch of longing, an inch of dust.*
> Burn a nuance in last lines. (Teng, 2006)

The lines in italics are translations of Li Shangyin's "无题 一" ["Untitled 1"], a poem from late Tang Dynasty about the persona's longing for his beloved. The poetic strategy here is reminiscent of that of the Language poets – the poem refuses to naturalize the lyrical expressivity of language. The lines skip back and forth from the scene of writing to the translation, highlighting the gap between the act of writing and writing as a lyrical meditation that has been translated. We are not even allowed to regard the act of writing as unmediated, for it is laden with laconic misreading ("He writes a scorched-earth policy"). The overall effect is one of defamiliarization. The poem refuses to read the translation – it refuses to enter into its lyrical expressivity. The lines "Torch what you want and can't take with you" may be read as a meta-commentary, reminding us that we cannot translate so easily, that we cannot translate and lay claim to an unmediated cultural inheritance and experience of poetry. The poem we see here renders visible the work of the translator: to translate a poem is to burn away the nuances of the poem.

Teng's poem interrogates the essentialist assumption that Singaporeans of Chinese ethnicity possess a form of immanent Chinese cultural knowledge that originates from their Chinese ancestry. Within the CMIO national imaginary, everyone in Singapore is effectively bilingual. As Rubdy argues, in Singapore, "there is multilingualism at the national level and bilingualism at the individual level in terms of official policy" (342). This goes against the reality that, as pointed out earlier, many creative writers that have emerged in Singapore are largely monolingual, or at least, are not as fluent in other languages as they are in English. One may suggest that the CMIO system places the burden of guilt on its citizens if they are not fluent in their Mother Tongues. Singapore's former prime minister, Lee Kuan Yew, had been known to make the following statement:

> I say a person who gets deculturalised – and I nearly was, so I know this danger – he loses his self-confidence. You feel a sense of deprivation. For optimum performance, a man must know himself, know the world. He must know where he stands. I may speak the English language better than I speak the Chinese language because I learnt English early in life. But I'll never be an Englishman in a thousand generations and I have not got the Western value system inside me; it's an Eastern value system with the western value system superimposed. (qtd. in Chua Chee Lay 126)

If Mother Tongues are normalized to be repositories of cultural knowledge, then one who is not fluent in any of them is constructed as a deculturalized being. Lee had started learning Mandarin at the age of 32 and Hokkien at 38 (Chua Chee Lay vii); his essentializing statement concerning language and deculturalization belongs to an earlier post-colonial and nation building framework that regards the English language as a colonial legacy misaligned with Singapore's cultural identity. (Yet this theme surfaced in many of his public speeches as well. There is the possibility that with the rising dominance of China in the world economy, Lee Kuan Yew's call to Chinese Singaporeans to reacquaint themselves with Mandarin may be seen as an act of cultural pragmatism.)

Hence, in an early poem, I dramatize the burden of cultural guilt imposed by Singapore's official nation building discourse:

A Second Language

I have never read proverbs on bamboo,
never felt the flourish of my name
in Chinese characters with the grip
and stroke of a brush. No calligraphy
records my genealogy. I know nothing,

though I recognise grandfather's face,
and recognise his father's face peering
from dusty portraits, and his father's
father's from a history book that records
my people flocking from a farther land.

My Mandarin becomes a second language
that fades like the memory of an old textbook.
I am familiar with only the Word and Cross
while *yin* and *yang* become superstition
just as herbs for wind are old wives' tales.

So now I study Chinese history
in English, commanding a feeble tongue
with the aid of *han yu pin yin*,
imitating melodious inflections,
like a child learning ABC's.

(Tay *Mental Life* 78)

In my first poetry collection, *Remnants*, there is a section called "Homage" where I re-write the poems of Li Bai, Du Fu and Li He. In my second collection, *A Lover's Soliloquy*, there is a sequence of poems called "Versions" which are mistranslations of Li Shangyin. My translations are, admittedly, reckless compared to Witter Bynner's faithful rendering of semantic content which corresponds to each line in the original:

To One Unnamed

You said you would come, but you did not, and you left me with no other trace
Than the moonlight on your tower at the fifth-watch bell.
I cry for you forever gone, I cannot waken yet,
I try to read your hurried note, I find the ink too pale.
...Blue burns your candle in its kingfisher-feather lantern
And a sweet breath steals from your hibiscus-broidered curtain.
But far beyond my reach is the Enchanted Mountain,
And you are on the other side, ten thousand peaks away. (Bynner 127)

From "Versions"

Coming and going
like an echo,
you carried away a promise
lodged deep in stone.

In the recesses of my mind
I see moonlight playing on rooftops,
hear the distance of a bell
and dream of you in another country...

I scribble a letter, though this is a longing
with no address.

Even as candlelight ignites these designs
of birds upon the quilt, the faint smell of musk
emerges from lotuses on my curtains.

Coming and going
like an echo,
you carried away a promise
lodged deep in stone.

I pause,
thinking of the distance of the hills.

(Tay *A Lover's Soliloquy* 27)

I am interested in re-reading and in the process, reclaiming an understanding of Tang Dynasty poetry without privileging an originary cultural moment. I read in order to write in my own language. As such, I dramatize the gap between the Tang classical tradition (7th to 10th century China) and the contemporary writing and reading scene in Singapore. Perhaps one should accept the paradox that infidelity is also an assertion of ownership.

I am reminded of the words of Red Pine (Bill Porter), the translator of the *Heart Sutra*, *Diamond Sutra* as well as the Cold Mountain poems, concerning the act of translation. I met him in May 2008 in Hong Kong when he was giving a talk on his encounters with Buddhist and Taoist hermit monks in China. He said to me that he thought of translation as a dance: the translator must not step on the feet of his author and mimic his steps; to do so is to place a burden on the partner, a burden the partner may not be prepared to accept, for it restricts the partner's movement. Rather, the translator dances with the author in his or her own way, sometimes keeping up with the author, at other times improvising so as to add to the dance, but essentially moving on his or her own volition as a dancer.

I am also reminded of the works of Wong Phui Nam, a Malaysian poet and a fellow mistranslator. Mistranslation in the case of Wong is a function of postcolonial and diasporic conditions. Wong writes that the first-generation immigrants who arrived in Malaysia (and this is also true of Singapore as well) "belonged to the poorest of the poor classes in their homelands" and hence, were "unburdened of the ancient classics, of religious insight, of the Confucian prescripts for correct social relationships, of poetry and letters, the fine arts and so on" (Wong 134). To mistranslate in this case is then to draw attention to the agency of the translators, to position translators as authors in their own right and hence highlighting their own literary environments. As Wong puts it, his mistranslations are ways of articulating "the Malaysian condition in ways [he] could not manage in [his] own verse" (86). He makes the point that "[a]ll [he] can claim for [his] versions is that they are personal readings of texts [he] like[s]" (86). Here, the line between translation and creative writing is blurred for we can read "Home Thoughts", his translation of Li Bai's famous poem, not just as expressing a longing to be home but also as expressing the poet-translator's sense of alienation from the socio-political landscape of Malaysia:

At my bed's feet my room ignites,
white with the moon's loneliness.
And I feel outside, the cold, incendiary
in the hard frost upon the ground.
I am full of the moon, on looking up,
hanging large above the window,
and in my dark, I meet, on looking down,
my fierce unsatisfied longing to be home. (Wong Phui Nam 80)

Wong, as a poet writing in English in Malaysia, experiences a triple alienation. While Singapore's multiculturalist policy leads to the reification of ethnic essences, Malaysia's nation building policies were such that they conferred a privileged status on those of Malay ethnicity. These policies were established after the Chinese-Malay race riots of May 1969, which occurred when it had become obvious that the Malay-dominant political parties were losing their hold on the government in the aftermath of the 1969 general elections. It has been observed that these policies "establish the superior Malay status through language, education, and economy" (Chin 6). In Malaysia, Malay is the official and national language. It is the medium of instruction in schools, though since 2003, because of the pressures of globalization, English is the medium of instruction for science and mathematics not just in the universities but in primary schools (Gill 249).

Hence, for Wong and his contemporaries, there is an official distinction between "national literature" which denotes works written in Malay, and "Sectional Literature" which denotes works in other languages (Fernando 138). I have mentioned elsewhere that: i) he is very much estranged from the official national literary canon, ii) he is not quite writing in the tradition of Chinese literature by virtue of his language choice, and (iii) he is, of course, not quite situated within the English literary tradition even though he writes in English (Tay "Unsettling Ways" 187). The poems he chose to translate often contain themes pertaining to alienation and disenchantment with the land. There is, then, a continuity to be found between Wong's poems and his translations.

What about a multilingual person who chooses not to translate or even mistranslate? Unlike Wong who still resides in Malaysia, Shirley Lim left for America soon after the 1969 race riots and is now a prominent scholar in the field of Asian American literature. For her, the use of the English language signifies a leave-taking:

It was more like cry,
a beloved country, and
see, traveler, on a hill,
by the wall, exchanging
what must be changed
forever, good-bye, farewell,
the different words working,
to say what is
unchangeable. Say, mother, father.
(Lim *Monsoon History* xxiv)

In an essay entitled "The Im/Possibility of Life-Writing in Two Languages", Lim makes the point that "[v]ery little of…polyglossic features [of Malaysia with its various languages and dialects] appear in [her] memoir, which, as a literary artefact, may therefore be said to be less real life than writing, albeit with the life in view" (44). Lim chooses not to negotiate between languages, neither to translate nor mistranslate, and acknowledges this lacuna in her writings.

Unlike Lim, I cannot ignore the various Chinese languages which are a part of the cultures of Singapore and Hong Kong, even though I do not have adequate written proficiency in Chinese. My mistranslations may be regarded, I hope, as an attempt at articulating an aspect of my identity that would otherwise be absent in one language. Translation is a bilingual experience at the very least, and living in Hong Kong, in close proximity to mainland China, I often wonder at the various linguistic experiences that differentiate and split up the experience of being Chinese. In Singapore, English is supposedly a culturally neutral language while Mandarin is supposedly a Mother Tongue. In contrast, the majority of Hong Kong people speaks Cantonese and is generally less proficient in English and Mandarin. The attitudes of Hong Kong people towards acquiring Mandarin are linked to their attitudes towards mainland China. As Chris Davison and Winnie Y. W. Auyeung Lai argue regarding the use of Mandarin (also known as Putonghua) as the medium of instruction in schools,

On the one hand Putonghua-medium programs are increasingly being chosen by socio-economically advantaged Hong Kong parents to develop their children as elite bilinguals who can transcend linguistic and cultural boundaries; on the other hand similar kinds of bilingual instruction are being rejected by poorer working class communities who associate Putonghua with the low status and conditions of mainland immigrants. (120)

These are the complications of moving between languages and Chinese cultures in its various social, national and geopolitical permutations.

The following poem is a testimony to the fractures that occur when one is negotiating between various ways of being Chinese. Who am I, given my privileged position as an academic from Singapore working in Hong Kong, to represent the voice of a sweatshop worker in mainland China? The following bilingual poem seeks to give voice to the worker even as it acknowledges its textual distillation of the subaltern's use-value:

Sweatshop Poem

This is a story, no,
this is a poem
about a noun that blazed her way
through my sentences.

She tore up the form book
and forgot the rules
and as a responsible writer,
I thought I should stop writing and suspend the event
because of safety fears.
[一对新人现身]

Or maybe she is waiting
for a married couple to appear,
maybe she wants to be translated into Chinese.

She was violent and angry
because she cannot be translated.

But in the end,
none needed to be admitted to hospital
even though there may have been a fire.

Maybe she is waiting
for 张国荣
her Leslie Cheung pop star romance lover
to appear like a verb
to her noun.

This sweatshop of a poem will not involve romance,
so she needs to do some real work.

But this writer, her current employer,
has fired two employees within seven days.

The noun tried to run away,
but was in trouble because she did not do her work
of making this poem make sense.

(Tay *Mental Life* 22-23)

LEARNING, TEACHING AND
THE PURSUIT OF CREATIVE WRITING
(WITH EVA LEUNG AS SECOND AUTHOR)

For writers, teaching is in itself a creative pursuit. We learn in order to teach, and we teach in order to learn. The experience of learning and teaching in the creative writing classroom is a prism through which we explore issues pertaining to the pursuit of creative writing. The first part of this section draws on my experience of creative writing classes conducted by Edwin Thumboo, who, as Shirley Lim puts it, "is the closest Singapore has to a poet laureate" (Lim, *Against the Grain* 22). It also looks at some of the works of the younger generation of writers in Singapore whose works emerged in the 1990s. The second part of this section draws on Eva Leung's (the second author) experience as a student of creative writing. It then looks at some of the issues germane to the literary scene in Hong Kong. The last section then outlines the implications of the above for teaching creative writing in Singapore and Hong Kong.

Hence, this is a work of conjoined autoethnography. We find autoethnography to be crucial to the documenting of the creative writing scenes in Singapore and Hong Kong, for it enables us to recognize the creative writing teacher and student as embedded within a web of relationships that pertain not only to literary texts and authors, but to the society at large and to some of the socio-political and as well language issues confronting Singapore and Hong Kong that register significantly on the individual level. We draw attention to our own situations not because we feel our positions to be exemplary or unique, but because we recognize that in order for us to fulfil and understand our roles as creative writers and teachers, we have to develop a vantage point from which we begin to critique and understand the culture, social relations, identity and social practice and values within which creative writing is immersed.

THE SINGAPORE LITERARY SCENE

There is a colonial slant to the literary curriculum in Singapore. For the Singapore literature student, literary works usually arrive fully formed from Anglo-American sources, first as titles on a course reading list and later as books in the bookstore. Literature in the Anglo-American traditions was and still is dominant in the literary curriculum in Singapore. In this respect, the practice of creative writing is often obscured from the average English major. Hence, Edwin Thumboo's creative writing class was something of a shock for me. It was something of a revelation that literary works were created in the same way as undergraduate essays. This is a point I bear in mind when I teach creative writing – there is a need on the part of the teacher to remove the aura of mystique attached to canonical literary works.

A major aspect of Thumboo's creative writing class has to do with cultivating the awareness of one's culture milieu and hence the need to dissociate one's writing from the Anglo-American literary canons even as one writes in English. As he puts it in his introduction to a poetry anthology:

> In a sense the language is remade, where necessary, by adjusting the interior landscape of words in order to explore and meditate the permutations of another culture and environment.
> (Thumboo *Second Tongue* ix)

The above passage gestures towards the notion of appropriation elaborated in *The Empire Writes Back*. Appropriation refers to a strategy of using English in such a way as to "maintain [one's] distance and otherness" from a cultural center so as to articulate one's cultural difference, hence creating a distinct national canon (Ashcroft 58). In a recent poem, Thumboo calls upon other younger poets to refresh the tradition:

> Recharge the canon, doubly with our voices;
> The recent one; some older have done their work.
> Distil our narrative; insert metaphor and icon.
> Speak that all may see us. Our needs are similar,
> Masuri, Yoon Wah, Kannabiran, Alvin, Lynette
> And others of our tribe. (Thumboo *Still Travelling* 83)

Indeed, Thumboo's role as a poet and university teacher cannot be overemphasized. As a teacher of creative writing, Thumboo is in a position to influence younger writers and hence help create a body of work that is able to bear the burden of Singapore's cultural experience. Cyril Wong (poet and novelist) and Alfian Sa'at (poet, short story writer, and playwright) are two prominent young writers in Singapore in their early thirties who attended Thumboo's creative writing class. At a session devoted to recognizing Thumboo's pivotal role in Singapore literature during the Singapore Writers Festival held in October 2009, the poets Alvin Pang and Aaron Lee spoke of a meeting they had with Thumboo shortly after their debut poetry collections were published in 1997. As they recalled, he asked them how he could support them in their endeavors. Hence, there is a sense that there is a Singaporean literary community.

Though there is a coherent body of writings known as Singapore literature, there is a clear internal demarcation between various generations of writers. The earlier generation of poets, as represented by Thumboo, Lee Tzu Pheng and Arthur Yap (whose work we will engage with later in the book), often engages with issues pertaining to national life and national belonging. Often-studied poems by Thumboo include "Ulysses by the Merlion", "Catering for the People" and "Island", which deal with the intertwined themes of statehood, national identity and multiculturalism. Lee's poem "My Country and My People" deals with the sense of disenchantment that accompanies urban life as defined by the state. In Yap's writings, there is a overriding concern with everyday life within Singapore's national space, as evidenced by poems such as "2 mothers in a h d b playground", "there is no future in nostalgia" and "old house at ang siang hill".

In contrast, as Gwee Li Sui argues, the generation of poets whose works emerged in the late 1990s "reposition the poets' emotions outside the discourses and urgencies of [national] belonging" (252). Furthermore, as Gwee argues, they are literary activists, in that they are proactive in terms of establishing literary journals and organizing local poetry events for readers and budding writers (Gwee 236). Creative writing as a practice for these authors is also a transnational practice. These younger authors are also active in terms of showcasing their works abroad by reading at literary festivals in Edinburgh, Austin and Hong Kong, among other cities. Transnational mobility is a pervasive theme in their works. Yong Shu Hoong's *Frottage* (2005) is a collection of poems based on his travels in Australia, while the works of Boey Kim Cheng, a former Singaporean, often engages with the theme of nomadic restlessness, as seen in the title of his memoir, *Between Stations* (2009).

This does not mean, however, that their works do not look back at Singapore. Alvin Pang's work as an anthologist is especially intriguing – the poetry volumes he edits are often the fruits of transnational collaborations. Examples include *Love Gathers All: The Philippines-Singapore Anthology of Love Poetry* (2002), *Over There: Poems from Australia and Singapore* (2008) and *Double Skin: New Poetic Voices from Italy and Singapore* (2009). In contrast, his anthology, *Tumasik* (2009), takes stock of Singapore's poetic oeuvre and it resists Singapore's state policy of multiculturalism. Singapore is a pluralistic society, and the state recognizes Chinese, Malay, Indian and Others as official ethnic and corresponding linguistic categories. In Singapore, English is the medium of instruction in schools, while students of each ethnic group attend their own Mother Tongue language lessons as a second language. As previously mentioned, there is a tendency for the CMIO system to be replicated in literary production. While the CMIO system supposedly allows for ethnic representation in a pluralistic society, the problem with the system is that it compartmentalizes the ethnic identities of Singaporeans.

Pang's anthology is conscious about resisting this segregationist effect, and *Tumasik* is an anthology that presents English translations of works written in Chinese, Malay and Tamil alongside those written in English. In the preface, Pang points out that "although this anthology is presented in English, its many voices do not conform to monocultural expectations: they swim between tongues, vernaculars, conventions and codes" (Pang *Tumasik* 18). The point is not that such a volume represents a defiance of state policy, for certainly such a strategy lends itself to a more sophisticated presentation of Singapore as a boutique multicultural nation. What is valuable about Pang's project is its conscious attempt at crossing linguistic and cultural divides internal to the nation so as to draw attention to the problematic of presenting in a single language the multi-lingual nature of literary production in Singapore.

Tumasik was supported by a publishing grant from the National Arts Council of Singapore (NAC) and it is part of a series of volumes put out by the International Writing Program at the University of Iowa. In this regard, Pang and the younger writers in Singapore are generally more transnational in terms of their literary vision. Without a doubt, the newer generation of writers is conscious of their location within the global literary community, as evidenced by the online literary journal *Quarterly Literary Review Singapore* which has been running since 2001. As mentioned in its mission statement, its "paradigms are the TLSes and LRBs of this world" ("About QLRS"). While the works of Thumboo, Lee and Yap were initially available to a small and elite university readership in Singapore, the literary activities of the current generation of younger writers are more global in scope. Supported by travel grants from NAC, they have read their works (sometimes as a Singaporean contingent) in international literary events in Edinburgh, Stockholm, Austin, Hong Kong, and elsewhere.

However, it has to be noted that even though some of the works of these younger writers articulate a certain measure of indifference, if not suspicion, towards the state's nation building agenda, their state-sponsored literary activities have found a global audience. This in turn resonates with the state's attempt at positioning Singapore as a global economic and cultural center on par with cities such as London and New York, as articulated in *The Renaissance City Report*, a cultural policy vision published by the Ministry of Information and the Arts in 2000 and updated in 2008.

THE HONG KONG LITERARY SCENE

There are certainly parallels to be drawn between the contemporary literary scenes in Singapore and Hong Kong. The online literary journal *Quarterly Literary*

Review Singapore has its younger Hong Kong counterpart in *Cha: An Asian Literary Journal*. There is also the *Asian Literary Review*, a quarterly print journal based in Hong Kong that features the works of emerging Asian-focused works alongside writers of international renown, such as Su Tong, Salman Rushdie and Mahmoud Darwish. The Singapore Writers Festival has its counterpart in the annual Hong Kong International Literary Festival which has been running since 2001. Between 2007 and 2012, prior to the sponsor's withdrawal of financial support, there was also the annual Man Asian Literary Prize, the sister prize to the Booker. The University of Hong Kong has a part-time and mid-residency MFA program in Creative Writing while the City University of Hong Kong had a low-residency MFA program in Creative Writing between 2010 and 2015. The City University of Hong Kong has since closed its program, citing the reason that there was insufficient student enrolment, while faculty and students claimed that this was in fact motivated by a wish to clamp down on the freedom of expression on the part of the authorities. In Singapore, Nanyang Technological University has a Creative Writing minor, a Master of Arts with specialization in Creative Writing, as well as PhD research with possible Creative Writing concentration. There are independent presses dedicated to publishing literary works by Singaporeans, such as Epigram Books, Ethos Books, Firstfruits Publications, Landmark Books and Math Paper Press. Most, if not all, literary works published by these presses were supported with NAC's publishing grants. In Hong Kong, Proverse Hong Kong and Chameleon Press, among other independent publishers, have been featuring literary works by authors based in Hong Kong. The Hong Kong Arts Development Council does sometimes provide publishing grants to these literary presses.

Eva Leung's (the second author) early encounter with creative writing as an undergraduate at the University of Hong Kong was when she was taking creative writing classes conducted by Shirley Geok-lin Lim, the Malaysian-born Asian American scholar and writer. It was during a one-to-one session with Lim that Eva first learned that, contrary to what she was told by a well-meaning teacher when she was in primary school, good poetry need not rhyme. By comparing Eva's poem which consisted of a forced rhyming pattern with greeting card verses, Lim demonstrated how rhymes could weaken a poem. In this session, and also in her lectures, Lim emphasized how the meanings of the poems and the content should come before the form and the rhyming scheme, which should only come naturally to complement the delivery of the central message.

In "English-Language Creative Writing in Hong Kong: Colonial Stereotype and Process", Lim mentions that, from her experience with Hong Kong students, they would "submit their work regularly, eagerly read [her] comments, and revise and rewrite *faithfully*" [emphasis added] (184). Her observation affirms Hong Kong students' need for an authoritative figure to tell them which parts they need to rewrite, and how they should do it. They have a tendency to obey those in authority, to the extent that even in creative writing classes, students regard the instructor's written remarks on the paper as rules to follow. Lim also mentions, in the same article, that none of the Hong Kong students she has taught has asked for an individual consultation "the way that [her] American students did" and there was no awareness on their part that they were able to forge a "unique relationship with the teacher" (184).

To be fair, Lim's article seeks to dispel the following four stereotypes that pertain to Hong Kong students: i) that they "can only learn by rote because of the poor teaching and the overreliance on exams and memorisation"; ii) that they are "alienated from the English language and reject the potential for cultural expression in English"; iii) that they "view education as strictly utilitarian and English as instrumental"; and finally, iv) that they are "chiefly interested in making money and are materialistic philistines" ("Colonial Stereotype" 179). However, just as one needs to resist and question these stereotypes of Hong Kong students, one needs to acknowledge that there are social, cultural and economic forces at work which bring about conditions amenable to the above forms of behavior and attitudes that are being stereotyped.

Perhaps one of the most important elements to Anglophone creative writing in Hong Kong has to do with the location of creative writing within a society that is premised on capital accumulation. Of course, this also applies elsewhere, but in Hong Kong, the situation is perhaps more pronounced, given the territory's rise to economic prominence first as a manufacturing base and later as a global financial hub. Louise Ho, regarded by many as Hong Kong's foremost Anglophone poet, has made the point that "Hong Kong society has nurtured sensibilities for stocks and shares and property prices rather than sensibilities in abstractions and aesthetics" ("Hong Kong Writing" 173). It is no exaggeration to say that the culture of Hong Kong is such that the overarching concern governing the populace's day-to-day pursuits has to do with socio-economic advancement and upward social mobility.

Cantonese remains the working language of a large proportion of the community in Hong Kong, and the acquisition of English as a second language is set against a social and cultural background that largely privileges economic rather than aesthetic endeavors. As Peter Tung, Raymond Lam and Wai King Tsang argue, "English has always played a pragmatic role in Hong Kong education" (441). They point out that Hong Kong students perceive the learning of English to be a necessity for "predominantly economic and career reasons" (Tung 443). Angel Mei Yi Lin concurs with this, and goes on to argue that this perception is partly a result of the demand on the part of business corporations: "Implicitly, it is assumed and asserted that education should produce a ready-made labor force for business corporations" (430). Lin has also pointed out that the majority of children in Hong Kong "live in a non-English speaking home, and social and cultural world" (432).

What this means, therefore, is that the acquisition of the English language derives from an instrumentalist and pragmatic agenda. Louise Ho argues that "Hong Kong writing in English has not yet reached a critical mass whereby it can claim nomenclature and locality" ("Hong Kong Writing" 176). Tammy Ho, one of the Hong Kong-born editors of *Cha*, has this to say regarding her choice of the English language over Chinese, her first language, as a primary medium of creative expression: "I have come to realize the foolishness of having an inferiority complex towards my relationship with the [English] language" (Ho "Writing in a Second Language"). The native Hong Kong poet writing in English has to negotiate with the fact that she has chosen English over Chinese as her medium of creative expression.

One of the features of English language creative writing in Hong Kong, then, is its relation to the Chinese language. It is in this way that Hong Kong poetry in English is necessary to be viewed as a function of bilingualism. Cantonese that is refined, as Louise Ho tells us,

> Creates a civilized space,
> Or a proper silence,
> Which was not there
> Before he spoke. (*Incense Tree* 60)

We have here a moment where Cantonese is celebrated in English. Such a linguistic negotiation is a function of the Hong Kong poet's nonnative status with regards to the language (and culture of English literature). Leung Ping-kwan, whose works are mainly in Chinese, has also written of moments during the writing process when he negotiates between the two languages:

> I started to write the poem in English first, but shifted halfway to Chinese and finished it, then I 'translated' it back to English. English first, then Chinese, then English. But the two languages must have tangled deeper in my mind (204).

In Leung's case, the English language in Hong Kong is associated with freedom from ideological indoctrination. For him, Hong Kong has been a cosmopolitan space of literary discoveries:

While in the late 1960s and 1970s when [the] Chinese Mainland still upheld Critical and Socialist Realism as the main doctrine for any kind of writing, I, in this city of Hong Kong at the edge of the mainland, wandered through the dubious magazine stalls in Central and Tsim Sha Tsui, discovered avant-garde and underground magazines from the outside world, and eventually discovered, through English translation, writers such as Kenzaburo Oe, Julio Cortarzar, Jan Kott, Jorge Luis Borges and Gabriel Garcia Marquez (Leung 199).

The need to negotiate between two languages (and cultures) evident in the works of Leung and Louise Ho is likewise visible in the work of younger poets such as Jennifer Wong, whose first poetry collection *Summer Cicadas* was published in 2006:

> Dickens, Hardy, Eliot and Gaskell.
> I read for their culture, hoping my reading
> To come more effortless with time, and practice,
> The way locals find it: a hobby, a native leisure.
>
> Daily I am reading and speaking
> Their mother tongue. I am learning
> To call the same things by new names.
> I must remember to translate the tense
> Or else they will not understand. Every week
> I call home. Mother can understand
> And speak in Chinese, a language oblivious of tense. (32)

Wong's poem articulates for us the situation of being bicultural and bilingual and its implications for the Hong Kong Anglophone creative writer. It speaks of a need for the student of literature to negotiate between the languages and cultures of England and Hong Kong.

Given the bilingualism of Hong Kong's creative writers, their English language writings hint at a corresponding set of works in Chinese (or Cantonese) that remains unwritten. Perhaps it is this reflexive awareness of one's bilingual situation that characterizes creative writing in English in Hong Kong. This is a theme we shall explore later.

TEACHING CREATIVE WRITING: SOME LESSONS

The creative writing teacher in Singapore and Hong Kong would have to keep in mind the above-mentioned social and cultural conditions, and this has implications for the teaching of creative writing in these two Asian localities. My experience with creative writing in both territories has allowed me to keep the following points in mind when teaching in Hong Kong.

First, there is a need to remove the mystique surrounding literary works, especially since much of the undergraduate literary curriculum in Hong Kong and Singapore is drawn from Anglo-American canons. There is a need for us to work against reification of Anglo-American works as "classics". There is a need for the young Asian writer to recognize that there is often a gap between the actual historical persons and the great authors we recognize today. There is a need to recover creative writing as a function of mediation, serendipity and contingency. It would be useful then, for teachers to introduce beginning creative writing students to the published facsimiles of, say, T. S. Eliot's draft manuscript of "The Waste Land" complete with Ezra Pound's annotations.

Second, there is a need to consider the relative situation of the English language creative writing in Singapore and Hong Kong. A large number of writers in Singapore who use English as the language of creative expression do not write in any other languages. In contrast, creative writers in Hong Kong, such as Tammy Ho and Jennifer Wong, are often able to communicate and write just as effectively, if not more effectively, in Chinese. This is often the case with creative writing students in Hong Kong. In this respect, an especially salient activity for beginning writers in Hong Kong would be to loosely translate Chinese poems into English so as to learn to regard English as a language of creative expression rather than solely as a tool for international business communication.

Third, there is a need to draw attention to creative writing as not just a solitary activity, but as an activity that is socially embedded, whether in the form of monthly poetry readings or in the form of a local (as well as an international) community that centers around print and Internet literary journals of quality. Attention may be drawn to these readings and journals at the beginning of the creative writing course so as to social component to creative writing. I often made it a point to encourage beginning students to submit their work to these journals so that the act of creative writing becomes a real project rather than a graded exercise in the classroom.

Finally, there is a need to consider the nature of sponsorship for creative writing. One can make an argument here that the National Arts Council in Singapore tends to support English language writing projects because of its perceived global marketability. Furthermore, the state tends to be the partial sponsor, if not the sole driving force, of literary festivals and creative writing publications in Singapore. One needs to consider the cultural policy of the state vis-à-vis the work of creative writing. How may creative writers benefit from the state support without compromising their creative agenda? In Singapore, the CMIO policy may facilitate as well as hinder creative writing in English, in that it encourages the view that English is the *lingua franca* of the world at the expense of overlooking the potential of drawing from the resources of other "local" and "ethnic" languages.

In the case of Hong Kong, creative writing ventures tend to be initiated mostly by private enterprises. The annual Hong Kong International Literary Festival which has been running for a decade and the (now-defunct) Man Asian Literary Prize used to have the sponsorship of Man Investments, the global hedge fund investments company which also sponsors the Man Booker Prize. I was previously involved in *Poemography*, a project that brings together poets and photographers from Hong Kong, Beijing and Shanghai to introduce photography and poetry writing (in both English and Chinese) to students in the three cities. The project was sponsored by the Swire Organisation for Youth Arts, which was founded by Swire Properties, a property developer in Hong Kong and the Chinese mainland. As we can see, the pursuit of creative writing is a socially embedded affair founded on various forms of community collaborations. If one may generalize, the level of support for creative writing in Hong Kong and Singapore signals the emergence, if not the ongoing development, of creative writing in the two regions, and this needs to be communicated to the beginning creative writing student to drive home the point that there is a larger social dimension to creative writing.

It is clear that the field of creative writing is embedded within the social and cultural spaces of local communities. Even as creative writing in the academy is becoming a global phenomenon, and even as a significant number of graduates of creative writing programs have garnered international fame as writers, there is a need for its practitioners and teachers to consider the embedded nature of their craft in the social and cultural spaces of their local communities. In the case of Singapore and Hong Kong, Anglophone creative writing has to address a number of issues that pertains to the status of the English language, the nature of sponsors of creative writing, as well as attitudes to creative writing vis-à-vis the norms and social expectations, for these are issues that will inform one's classroom practice.

CURRICULUM AS CULTURAL CRITIQUE

As we have seen earlier, the practice and teaching of creative writing do not operate in a cultural vacuum. Hong Kong is regarded as an international city, a key Asian tourist destination and a center of high finance – all of that brooks no contention. Once we go beyond these surface descriptors, however, we begin to uncover a complex of political, cultural and linguistic situations that form the basis of the everyday life of Hong Kong people. Hong Kong identity is a fraught issue that has to do with its history as a former British colony as well as its current unique political configuration as one of two Special Administrative Regions (SAR) under the People's Republic of China, the other being Macau. The social-political configuration of Hong Kong is a political exception to mainland China, possessing, apart from its own currency, a relatively autonomous political structure (though this is of course subject to influence from Beijing.) That the SAR arrangement will dissolve in 2047 in accordance with the constitution of the Hong Kong Basic Law is a constant reminder of this state of temporary political exception.

Because Hong Kong Basic Law guarantees a degree of rights to the freedom of expression, one which grants its people a degree of freedom of political expression not found in mainland China, it continues to be a site of mass street demonstrations against China's human rights violations. It is a political space where personal lives, hopes and ambitions confront Beijing's official visions of the territory. What are some of the obligations a government may claim of its subjects, and to what extent is this congruent with individual understandings of allegiance from the people of Hong Kong? Here, we draw attention to a question Madeleine Slavick poses in her poem "Monday, June 4, 2001, Hong Kong":

> what is our duty
> to this Motherland,
> tonight, tonight, what do we give? (43)

The annual Victoria Park candlelight vigils commemorating the victims of the June Fourth Tiananmen Square tragedy continue to have record turnouts of more than a hundred and fifty thousand. Incidents pertaining to the incarcerations of various political activists such as Liu Xiaobo, Ai Weiwei and Chen Guangcheng have provoked mass street protests in Hong Kong.

In his analysis of a survey of political participation in Hong Kong, Francis L. F. Lee argues that "Hong Kong people's support for democratization is driven by a sense of the ability of the public as a collective actor more than by a sense of the individual himself or herself as a competent actor in the public arena" (307). One may translate this to mean that political activism in Hong Kong as represented by demonstrations and protests is motivated and defined in terms of a collective agency, and this collective agency may in turn be identified as a sense of nationhood. The paradox regarding Hong Kong's political activism is summed up in Louise Ho's poem "Remembering 4th June, 1989":

> We thought as one,
> We spoke as one,
> We too have changed, if "not utterly"
> And something beautiful was born. (*Incense Tree* 39)

Ho's allusion to W. B. Yeats' poem is significant. The comparison with the Easter Rising implies that Hong Kong's postcolonial nationhood was provoked into existence by the Tiananmen massacre:

> As we near the end of an era
> We have at last
> Become ourselves.
> The catalyst
> Was our neighbour's blood. (*Incense Tree* 39)

Benedict Anderson's notion of the nation as an "imagined community", a concept explored earlier, may be employed to understand Hong Kong's nationhood. As he argues, the community is "*imagined* because the members of even the smallest nation will never know most of their fellow-members, meet them, or even hear of them, yet in the minds of each lives the image of their communion" [italics in original] (Anderson 6). Anderson's notion is especially relevant to Hong Kong because even though there is no such thing as Hong Kong citizenship, one could nevertheless speak of a Hong Kong nation that exists in the mind of its people. In Ho's poem, with its echoes of Irish nationalism, Hong Kong's postcolonial moment was initiated by events outside of Hong Kong. In 1989, Hong Kong was on its way to becoming a nation despite its official as status a British colony, eight years prior to its sovereignty being transferred from the British to the Chinese. Indeed, dates are important to poems commemorating June Fourth – while Ho's poem is dated (or titled) 1989 as a direct historical allusion, the date given in the title of Slavick's poem, which we have seen earlier, is 2001, implying that the June Fourth Tiananmen Square tragedy continues to resonate in the political minds of the Hong Kong people. To put this in another way: in Hong Kong, political demonstrations against human rights issues in mainland China are on-going manifestations of the Hong Kong nation, a nation that has coalesced around memory of June Fourth.

Hong Kong's cultural situation may be understood as a further extension to its political condition. Hong Kong has never been in command of its sovereignty — in other words, its colonial history and its political present is that of dispossession. This sense of dispossession may be encapsulated in the bitterly ironic classification in Hong Kong in the 1980s of the nationality known as "British National (Overseas)". The BN(O) passport allows its holder to travel, but it does not grant him or her the right to live and work anywhere in the world, including Hong Kong, the United Kingdom, and mainland China. With this passport, one could travel anywhere, yet one has no right of abode. In his poem "BN(O)", Kit Fan writes of the queue for the passport as a line of "refugees longing for an identity / foreign to this tiny, floating, motherless city" that is Hong Kong (27). Hong Kong is a nation without citizenship. Seen in this light, the international and cosmopolitan nature of Hong Kong may be construed as composed of anxiety that pertains to its future. Perhaps this explains the cosmopolitan tendencies in Hong Kong cultural productions, in that time and again, there is a interpellation of the Hong Kong culture as that which is located at the intersections of (usually first) world cultures.

We see in Hong Kong's cultural sphere a cosmopolitanism without a firmly entrenched locality. It is rather interesting to note that many of Hong Kong's cultural and literary figures are peripatetic. Louise Ho, whose poetry we have seen earlier, now lives in Australia and visits Hong Kong occasionally. The younger poet Kit Fan lives in York while another younger poet, Jennifer Wong, is based in London. Xu Xi, whose work we shall look at later, was born in Indonesia and travels between Hong Kong and New York. This globalized mobility extends to prominent media personalities as well. Jackie Chan and Chow Yun-fat shuttle between Hong Kong and Hollywood. Indeed, one may plot a generalized trajectory with their character roles and media personalities. In the case of Jackie Chan, there is the kung-fu genre of the downtrodden pugilist who later acquires outstanding martial arts skills which allow him to defeat evil and greedy men in power (*Snake in the Eagle's Shadow*, *The Drunken Master*). There is also the Hong Kong policeman involved in international intrigues (*Rumble in the Bronx*, the *Rush Hour* film series) set in America. The rags-to-riches underdog narrative encapsulated in many of Chan's roles is conflated with the worldly man comfortable in various cosmopolitan settings, ranging from America (as previously mentioned) and Japan (*Shinjuku Incident*) to South Africa and the Netherlands (*Who Am I?*). In the case of Chow Yun-fat, from his early movies right up to *The Replacement Killers* (1998) and *The Curse of the Golden Flower* (2006), as Eric Kit-wai Ma argues, he "is utilized as an office worker, a romantic hero, a killer, a lover, a Chinese Hollywood star and a Chinese Emperor" (45). As such, his roles are "intermingled with the socio-psychological needs of Hong Kong society at large" (Ma 45). Transnational mobility extends to Hong Kong's urban space as well. David Clarke has argued that Hong Kong's urban landscape often contain echoes of other cities. For example, the curved roof of the Hong Kong Convention and Exhibition Centre, he argues, echoes those of the Sydney Opera House (Clarke 192-194), while the Hong Kong Cyberport is an attempt at replicating the success of Silicon Valley (Clarke 198). Hong Kong culture is forever looking elsewhere, outside, and beyond itself.

If *Angelus Novus* as painted by Paul Klee and wonderfully read by Walter Benjamin is one that is "[propelled]...into the future to which his back is turned", then one may posit an Angel of Necessity for the Hong Kong people, one that looks to the past even as it is compelled to leave it behind (Benjamin *Illuminations* 258). Transnational mobility is part of a larger phenomenon examined by Aihwa Ong in her book *Flexible Citizenship: The Cultural Logics of Transnationality*. For Ong, the term "'Flexible citizenship' refers to the cultural logics of capitalist accumulation, travel, and displacement that induce subjects to respond fluidly and opportunistically to changing political-economic conditions" (6). In the case of Hong Kong, flexible citizenship and its resultant transnational mobility are linked to a largely pragmatic and a prevalent matter-of-fact mindset that privileges instrumentality as a response to the sense of dispossession.

This pragmatic mindset is at work as well when it comes to the status of the English language in the territory. Hong Kong's post-1997 official language policy is that of biliteracy (English and Chinese) and trilingualism (English, Cantonese and Putonghua). Cantonese remains the most widely used language in everyday life, while the importance of Putonghua (given Hong Kong's relationship with mainland China) and English (given Hong Kong's colonial past as well as the notion that English is the *lingua franca* of the globalized world) in the minds of the people of Hong Kong cannot be denied. As Mee-Ling Lai argues in her study of the attitudes of Hong Kong students towards English, Cantonese and Putonghua,

> [t]heir attitudes towards the three languages remain positive with English being the most useful language for academic and career development, Cantonese being their mother tongue and the language of their local identity, and Putonghua the language for nation-wide communication and the sense of "Chineseness". (130)

Despite this, however, anecdotal evidence suggests that there is a bifurcation in language use in that the ordinary Cantonese-speaking Hong Kong person tends to be less fluent in English, a language associated with *gweilos* (a commonly used Cantonese slang for Caucasians). As a rule of thumb and as an indication of the English language proficiency of the everyday Hong Kong person, it is always a good idea for English-speaking *gweilos* either to be ready to enunciate the destination name in Cantonese or to have it on paper in Chinese characters when boarding a taxi.

The point is that the English language is regarded as instrumental to academic and career prospects rather than a language that is at the heart of one's identity. One needs to be wary of overgeneralization, but based on several years of my experience as an Undergraduate Admissions Convenor and an interviewer of candidates applying to major in English in my department which offers courses in Applied English Linguistics and English Literary Studies, it is fair to say that the majority of the candidates are drawn to the course of study because they regard English "as the *lingua franca* of the business world". This is a point made by approximately 70 per cent of the candidates in one form or another during the undergraduate admissions interviews conducted by my department. Only a minority of our undergraduate English majors have taken up English literature previously as an examinable subject in public examinations, though this is not the same as to say that they are unfamiliar with literary studies (given that they are at least familiar with Chinese literature).

While there is a small body of English language literary writing in Hong Kong, an interest in Hong Kong literature in English is at best regarded as a niche endeavor in the minds of the Hong Kong public. In his book *Hong Kong: Culture and the Culture of Disappearance*, Ackbar Abbas observes that "It takes a certain kind of determination for someone in Hong Kong to persist in the project of writing poems in English", given that the language of everyday discourse in Hong Kong is Cantonese (123). Abbas' argument regarding Hong Kong culture is that it possesses what he calls "a culture of disappearance" (7). What he implies by the phrase is "Not that there was nothing going on in cinema, architecture, and writing; [but that] it was just not recognized to be culture as such" (6). This argument is especially trenchant today, fifteen years after it was first made, as it was then.

Abbas has written of Louise Ho that her poetry bears evidence of coming to terms with the cultural environment of Hong Kong through English literature: "English literature functions less as a form of poetic authority than as a convenient grid against which the metastasizing habitations of the local can be situated" (125-126). Perhaps it is only now that we could further develop Abbas' argument as it pertains to the literary scene. One might say that the entrenched local condition of Hong Kong's English language literary scene is always transient and international in character. As a creative writer, I have been involved, at one time or another, with various literary collectives. There are at least two English language literary readings that occur monthly with overlapping memberships and audiences. The Poetry OutLoud collective, which has been running for more than a decade, meets on every first Wednesday of the month at the Fringe Club, an arts venue. Kubrick Poetry, established since 2007, has been meeting regularly at Kubrick Bookstore and Café, a noted independent bookstore that specializes in Hong Kong art, design and films. The majority of the attendees and participants are Caucasian expatriate residents in the education and publishing professions. Additionally, there is a small group of regular attendees who have returned from overseas studies. Many Hong Kong-based authors have launched their books at these readings. *Cha: An Asian Literary Journal* is a Hong Kong-based literary e-journal (at which I am currently serving as reviews editor) which focuses on Asian writing that has contributors from all over the world. Hence, even as the local is dispossessed politically, historically and culturally, the English language literary scene in Hong Kong is a local site around which a transnational literary community is formed and where literary and imaginative worlds are mapped out in English.

In her memoirs *Evanescent Isles*, Xu Xi writes of a linguistic experience which though in this case is perhaps somewhat embellished, nonetheless conveys a sense of what language use in Hong Kong is like between people of different cultural backgrounds, whereby actors are often presented as attempting to communicate across cultures and languages:

> I have a Cantonese friend with whom I converse. This should be an oxymoron in this city, because how else do we converse with friends except in Cantonese or "Canto-Ching-lish"? But this friend is unique because we converse in a Cantonese that is both our "native-but-not-exactly-first" language, and our friendship comprises these conversations that occur because I visit his bookshop, one that specializes in Chinese art. When Cantonese fails us, he reaches for a Putonghua (Mandarin) equivalent and I for English, at which point we consult one of the many dictionaries on his shelves. His spoken English is halting, limited to words or phrases, and my spoken Putonghua is clumsy, often lost in translation; we both read better than we speak each other's "native" language. Of course, since the handover [of Hong Kong to China in 1997], our city is supposed to be tri-lingual, claiming Cantonese, Putonghua and English as our tongues, or so the government claims. (Xu 38)

In this respect, English becomes the meta-language, a point of departure from which to map out transcultural and trans-linguistic moments unique to Hong Kong. The literary space is one in which an author could describe the actual lifeworld of language use against the official inscription of bi-literacy and tri-lingualism. As Elaine Ho points out, the "global horizons [of writers in Hong Kong] are neither defined by the British Empire nor the anglophone West" (435). Ho's point is the culmination of what the work of sociolinguists such as Kingsley Bolton has been arguing. Bolton has drawn attention to what he calls the "myth of monolingualism", in that while it is a commonly held notion that members of a society is essentially monolingual, the sociologist actually finds abundant evidence of multilingualism in everyday language use (Bolton 274-275). With reference to encounters such as the one narrated by Xu Xi as above, we could make the argument, as Alan Firth has done, that language competence involves a "mastery of strategies for the accomplishment of accommodation of diverse practices and modes of meaning" which in this case, take place within a cosmopolitan setting (163). The paradox of Hong Kong's English language literary culture, as one may surmise from the above passage taken from Xu Xi's work, is that its autochthonic trait lies in its being international in character.

THE AIM OF A CRITICAL PEDAGOGY: LANGUAGE AS A FIELD OF THOUGHT

We have seen earlier how the English language is regarded by Hong Kong students as crucial to their academic and career prospects. As Douglas Kerr points out, English language writers in Hong Kong are pitted not so much against Chinese language authors or even "the Great Tradition of English [literature]", but against a kind of hollowed-out and functional English:

> For there is a kind of English that is a prized commodity precisely because it is a-local; it goes everywhere and belongs nowhere… This tumbleweed English is entirely instrumental, an English for data and proposals and sales pitches but not for ideas, for negotiating postures and "social talk" but not arguments and conversations… [A]nyone who has been into an English-language bookshop in Hong Kong or scanned the advertisements for tutorial schools (or indeed met some Hong Kong students) will know that this is what many want from English. (88)

The association between English language and the notion of globality segues easily into an instrumentalist approach to the study of English. Kerr's point raises a question: how is one to distinguish between English as a global international and "a-local" language, and the language of Hong Kong authors who are, in the words of Elaine Ho as mentioned above, "neither defined by the British Empire nor the anglophone West" (435)?

On the one hand, we have English as an "a-local" language. This is the English one needs to have in order to pass one's language examinations or for a career in international finance and business. This is the kind of English (combined with the way in which education is perceived as a path to upward social mobility in Hong Kong) that has engendered celebrity private tutors whose annual salaries are calculated in the millions and whose faces are seen on billboards, posters and TV commercials. On the other hand, we have English as a function of English-language literary local culture in Hong Kong with global horizons – is there a difference?

Perhaps one may distinguish between what one might call a prosaic as opposed to a poetic use of English. The prosaic approach is a pragmatic approach, one that regards language as a means to various ends. The poetic approach regards language as an end in itself – it is not necessarily about poetry, but it claims English as a subjective terrain from which one makes sense of the world. By this, I mean English as a language that enables sense, meaning and thought, a language not so much comprising of objects and objectives to be attained, but, as Derek Attridge says of a text, as "something like a field of potential meaning awaiting realization without wholly determining it in advance" (25). This, I argue, is the necessary and perhaps urgent aim of critical pedagogy in the Hong Kong context. This is where the teaching of creative writing has an important role to play, in that it resists the capitalist over-determination of everyday life in a city such as Hong Kong, which is dominated by the twin industries of high finance and property.

This is where we turn to the work of Paulo Freire. His work has important resonances for intellectual and social movements that interrogate the status quo; as he describes it, it has implications for both "laborers (peasant or urban) and… middle-class persons" (Freire 37). A broad definition of critical pedagogy would entail an element of self-reflexivity on the part of both the students and teachers. Whatever the content that is being taught, there has to be an undercurrent of thought that asks questions about how the content and the way in which it is taught and valued by society works for or against inherent power structures and their prevalent ideological biases, alongside the potential for transformation and enfranchisement, whether personal or social. Importantly, Freire's work draws attention to the importance of consciousness-raising in classroom situations, reminding us that there is no such thing as an ideologically-free educational setting (Shaull 34).

There are various moments in Freire's work that are especially relevant to the task of creative writing. First, in a section on the importance of dialogue, there is an emphasis on the authenticity of one's language: "There is no true word that is not at the same time a praxis. Thus, to speak a true word is to transform the world" (Freire 87). How, then, does one arrive at an authentic word? One of the ways to do so is by regarding language not as objects and objectives to be attained. There is a need to depart from the prosaic and instrumentalist attitude as discussed previously and instead, to approach language not with the agenda of mastery but with a degree of openness that allows for difference. As we shall see in student writing samples later, an important theme to creative writing has to do with how it differs from the writing of academic essays. This difference, which allows for the affective expression of a personal vision, aligns the work of creative writing with the act of articulating (and hence fostering) an imagined community.

Second, drawing from Erich Fromm's work, Freire elaborates on distinction between "biophily" and "necrophily" within the educational context (77). Necrophily refers to the preservation of the dead, the maintenance of socio-political culture, while biophily refers to a life of consciousness and deliberation, one which privileges agency, autonomy and communication with the world. Again, this is an important topic that is addressed by student reflections on creative writing which regards the English language as a space of emergence and potentiality rather than solely as a passport to upward social mobility.

Last, Freire draws attention to how society determines the professional roles of its individuals: "Professional women and men of any specialty, university graduates or not, are individuals who have been 'determined from above' by a culture of domination which has constituted them as dual beings." (158). They are dual beings because, on the one hand, by virtue of their positions, they have worked with and accepted the norms of society; on the other hand, their professional abilities may become "an instrument for the transformation of culture" (Freire 159). This notion of dual beings has important consequences for the consideration of what it is that we could accomplish as teachers of creative writing located within higher institutions of learning. The potency of Freire's work is such that we cannot walk away from an encounter without considering our specific situation as educators. A teacher of creative writing is not just an educator in a university; as someone committed to the writing arts, he or she understands the value of writing in itself, apart from any valuation according to the norms of a capitalist-oriented society. As discussed previously, creative writers employed by universities are in an ironic situation because even though they recognize that they do not quite fit in with institutional hierarchies, they understand that the academic industry (which includes creative writing programs) is a source of tuition dollars that facilitate their creative pursuit. Universities and creative writing programs represent money for art's sake.

The creative writer is located within the collective Hong Kong mythology of higher education and the English language as passports to better (read cosmopolitan) life. This mythologization (or what Roland Barthes calls "robbery by colonization") is such that the English language and higher education is naturalized (and commoditized) as the path to opportunities in a capitalist-oriented lifeworld (Barthes *Mythologies* 132). This is alluded to in the following passage taken from a class assignment that requires the creative writing students to consider what creative writing means to them. (I should note here that permission has been sought and granted by my students to quote their work, as long as anonymity is preserved. The parenthesis in the text replaces the student's actual name):

> … when I am writing academic essays, I feel that I am trading my talents and betraying my "self" in order to pass the courses and obtain a good G.P.A. I feel that the ["I"] who writes academically is just created, unwillingly, within the constraints of life. The real "me" does not write in that way as I at heart understand that I love resplendent words with emotion and pulchritude. Creative writing, therefore, has a chaste and sacred place in my heart. It is a moral high ground which keeps me from following the flow of people who have no souls and feelings in their life, like tins of sardines to be consumed as a corollary.

The implicit dichotomy between the writing of academic essays as prostitution and creative writing as chaste is hard to miss here. The writing of academic essays is part and parcel of "the constraints of life", referring to the necessity of obtaining good grades as part of a larger causal chain between academic work and job prospects. Creative writing, on the other hand, is a depository of the "real" self that is barred from academic writing. Another student has this to say:

I enjoy writing poetry as I do not need to care about others' opinion or judgment when writing it as much as I do in other types of writings. The best example is its difference between an essay and a poem. For essays, you need to be convincing. You need to take into the perspective of others and question yourself if the points you made are logical or not. You cannot be too sentimental when expressing your own opinion. Although poetry is also a sequence of words with rhetoric, I feel that as long as I can convince myself, it is reasonably a good piece of writing already.

Again, there is a dichotomy here: academic essays are a form of writing for others, while creative writing (or poetry) constitutes a dialogue with and for the self. In both passages, we witness a critical attitude that appreciates the differences between academic and creative writing. It is in creative writing that is associated not with the agenda of having to demonstrate one's mastery but with a degree of attention to the self that allows for difference.

Of course, what we need to recognize is that this is a false dichotomy on a few counts. First, there is the assumption that creative writing is free from the kind of constraints that academic essay writing is under, for creative writing is also assessed, though with a different (and more fluid) set of criteria. Second, regarding the notion that creative writing allows for the real self to emerge, one may argue that the self that emerges from creative writing is no less authentic than the self that emerges from writing academic essays – both selves are, after all, textual constructs. Finally, there is the Romantic belief that creative writing is a valid and rewarding path to meaning, autonomy and agency. As educators who are at the same time creative writers, this is a belief close to our heart. However, perhaps one is too quick to assume that those without literary and/or aesthetic inclinations are "people who have no souls and feelings in their life", shorn of meaning, autonomy and agency.

Creative writers in institutions of higher learning operate with a degree of irony. On the one hand, creative writing is easily regarded as the depository of the self; on the other hand, as an academic endeavor, it is embedded, just like traditional academic courses, with an apparatus of assessment. Creative writing is both biophily and necrophily; it promises a life of consciousness in as much as it is involved with the maintenance and preservation of a rigid hierarchy of assessment. Alastair Pennycook has argued that "education needs to proceed by taking account of student knowledge, identity and desire" (41). While Pennycook was referring to how educators need to be aware of popular culture and its influence in language education, he also makes the point that language is also about the "production of identity" (30). This is where the creative writers and academics, as dual beings, have a role to play. On the one hand, the subject position of the creative writer in a university is determined from above, from authority, mastery and power. On the other hand, there is that promise of openness associated with creative writing that the creative writer and academic could cling to, such that that would be a space of possibilities that is being articulated. What may such a space of possibility look like? The creative writing classroom, then, may be that space of consciousness-raising, of a field of potential, of a preparation for the emergence of difference.

CREATIVE WRITING PEDAGOGY: CULTURAL CRITIQUE AND CULTURE AS RESOURCE

The creative writing teacher, if he or she is of a different cultural and national background, would have to consider some of his or her own cultural assumptions. We have explored previously the significance of autoethnographic consciousness that one brings to the task of creative writing. As someone born in Singapore and having lived in my birth country for close to three decades before arriving in Hong Kong, I am fully conscious of how matters pertaining to culture, language and identity are subject to organic historical and social forces in as much as they are subject to conscious cultural policing on the part of the state. The cultural landscape of Singapore has undergone a vast transformation due to an educational system that adopts English as the medium of instruction. Depending on the ethnicity of the student, he or she would study Mandarin, Malay or Tamil which are officially designated as Mother Tongue language subjects. This is part of a pragmatic cultural policy which aims to equip Singaporeans with the ability to engage with an increasingly globalized landscape that has English as its *lingua franca*, and at the same time provide a linguistic base on which one could depend to foster a sense of (ethnic) belonging within a (multicultural) nation. As Chua Beng Huat has argued, Singapore's official ethnic categories of Chinese, Malay, Indian and Others is a way of managing the plurality of cultures and languages within the tiny nation-city-state ("Multiculturalism in Singapore" 60). Even this situation is undergoing a sea-change in recent years, as Singapore's aggressive immigration policy has resulted in a large presence of recent migrants from mainland China, South Asia and different parts of Southeast Asia which complicates the CMIO model.

In the case of Hong Kong, the influx of migrants from the Chinese mainland, as well as its status as a financial hub which relies on a pool of expertise from people from developed Anglophone countries, has resulted in a multilingual landscape with Cantonese, Mandarin and English as its dominant languages. The English-language creative writing teacher of Chinese ethnicity from Singapore situated in the Department of English at the Chinese University of Hong Kong is a position nested within multiple linguistic and national zones. This is an awareness that could only arise when one juxtaposes the cultural complexities of one's identity as a function of his or her birth country with that of the country and institution in which he or she finds himself or herself. We have seen in the above Abbas argument that Hong Kong culture was not recognized to be culture as such. To the contrary, for the creative writer teacher who hails from another place, one sees culture wherever one looks. Hence, one of the ways to enable the task of creative writing in the Hong Kong classroom is to draw upon the complexities of culture as a resource.

It has always been my practice in the classroom to externalize the creative writing process. By this, I mean that, rather than regarding the work of creative writing as "expressing one's self", students are tasked to go through a series of previously prepared exercises that take them outside of themselves and shut down any tendency towards introspection. Depending on the nature of the exercise, such a move would then compel the budding writer to draw from the culture of Hong Kong for the composing of the poem. The following stanzas, from a student's poem entitled "A Mute in the Modern City", are a result of an exercise that requires the writer to model their writing after a poem of their choice. In this case, the student has chosen to model her poem after Louise Ho's "Jamming":

> They call it a "red-coated fish" here.
> Perhaps it lets you swim through doors,
> Full of authority,
> Just like its name in English
> - A Cardinal.
> NO MONEY NO TALK

> Trust me it's true,
> When local kids shout in ensemble
> "IT'S NOT BLUE IT'S NOT BLUE!"
> See how they grin
> From deep within;
> When they find those little red fishes
> Swimming inside the red packets.
> NO MONEY NO TALK

But it gets fishy,
When those from the North,
Go into Gucci, Chanel and D&G,
Carrying bundles of dried red fishes
In their suitcases.
The salesmen greeted them with a smile,
While I was scanned from bottom to top.

NO MONEY NO TALK

The references make sense only if one is familiar with Hong Kong. The "red-coated fish" (*hong sam yu*) is a colloquial reference to the Hong Kong hundred-dollar bill, and local kids do not wish to see blue in their red packets because blue is the color of a twenty-dollar note. Red packets are monetary gifts usually given from adults to children during Chinese New Year festivities. The poem is making a point about how children are conditioned to be sensitive to monetary value at a young age. The line "those from the North" refers to mainland Chinese tourists and business people who are flocking to Hong Kong, and the poem is suggesting that their "fishy" wealth is obtained from suspicious sources. This is a poem which, by virtue of its cultural allusions, testifies to the availability of shared symbols (such as the "red-coated fish") that characterizes the imagined community of Hong Kong. This is also an anxious poem that makes a point about how the already materialistic culture of Hong Kong is exacerbated by the arrival of the *nouveau riche* from mainland China.

The fact that is it a poem modelled after Louise Ho's "Jamming" makes it more poignant. The following stanzas from "Jamming" exemplify the persona's irreverent attitude towards his or her interlocutor's attempt at correcting the persona's cultural ignorance:

An oaf pretending to things intellectual
Stamping and stammering pronounced
"Beauty
Is in the eye
Of the beholder"

geeleegulu

The editor crossed out Menteth
To put in Macbeth, carelessness
Or plain be-loo-dy ignorance

geeleegulu

"Ooooh, do you think
She can tell the difference
Between irony and mere cliché"

(Louise Ho *Incense Tree* 42)

"Jamming" is a work of postcolonial cultural jamming, whereby colonial intellectual pretensions are interrupted and disdainfully labelled "*geeleegulu*", a Cantonese colloquialism meaning "gibberish". The contrast between Ho's "Jamming" and the student's poem is stark – while Ho's refrain is a Cantonese colloquialism denoting an irreverent attitude towards what is being articulated, the refrain in "A Mute in the Modern City" indicates that the persona is silenced because of his or her lack of wealth. Perhaps the poem is suggesting that Hong Kong which was the last British colony is now colonized by the emerging new mainland Chinese empire of wealth. The irreverent Hong Kong persona ("*geeleegulu*") is now reduced to silence by the power of mainland Chinese capital ("NO MONEY NO TALK"). As it draws from a Hong Kong poem in order to perform an immanent cultural critique, this is one of the more powerful and culturally autochthonous of poems which have emerged from the creative writing course. There is evidence, then, to show that there are attempts to go beyond the treatment of language as a functional tool for upward social mobility. There is, as the poem "A Mute in the Modern City" demonstrates, a locally embedded form of English language put to creative use which is a testimony to the imagined community of Hong Kong.

Another conscious decision I have taken in the course is to regard creative writing not only as a solitary endeavor, but as a social activity, and to remind the students of how writing is an endeavor embedded within literary circles, inhabited by editors, publishers and interested audiences. In other words, I would make the point that students need to be socialized into the act of writing. Hence, a student wrote of his experience of meeting poets at a Poetry OutLoud session whose works he has encountered in the journal *Cha*:

> I was present in the poetry-reading session in Fringe Club in Central for a few times. They are all very welcoming and even though I am just a student, I feel comfortable to be in the club, being a part of them. In some occasions, students like me will be welcomed to share their poems on stage in front of all the writers. Their unfailing support and advice for the new-era writers are a significant impetus for the new writers or students who are interested in writing to continue composing. Therefore, it seems to me that the journal

is basically a community in which writers share their ideas and writings harmoniously. It nourishes the relationship among writers of different nationalities. It is a sharing of joy.

This is a passage about a sense of community, about sharing, about biophily. While there is much one could learn from a literary course on modernism or the Romanticism, I believe a creative writing class has to draw attention to the notion that writing is a social event. An undergraduate course on, say, Romanticism or the modernists would no doubt be able to draw attention to the friendships, collaborations and camaraderie among writers that had existed which gave birth to the literary movements, but these would perhaps be understated compared to the emphasis that is rightfully given to textual explication and close reading. Creative writing at the undergraduate level on the other hand would be well-placed as a course that draws attention to the social aspects of literature, allowing them to tap into the networks of collaborations, friendships and rivalries that exist among a community of editors, publishers and writers. There would then be that social support, introducing real life experience into an academic endeavor. Hence, when we are working on an exercise in providing peer critique, there is that additional awareness that such feedback occurs all the time between writers, editors and publishers outside the classroom. In this respect, the classroom becomes a microcosm of the community of social actors that exists in Hong Kong's cultural space.

I am hopeful of the outcome of the creative writing classroom. A majority of the students might gain an insight into the act of writing creatively, and a small number (usually two to three per class in a course that runs once a year) would be committed to the art of writing and be involved in the literary community. A postgraduate teaching assistant of the course worked as a volunteer at the Hong Kong International Literary Festival. An undergraduate student sought employment in the private sector upon graduation but realized later she wanted to further her interests in creative writing, and had joined an MFA program in the UK. A third student who aimed to be an English language teacher in a Hong Kong secondary school realized he has the resources and experience now to foster an interest in creative writing in his future students. Yet another had found her first employer, a small English language independent literary press, through one of the literary readings she frequented. Two of our former undergraduates who had taken the creative writing course had been invited to read their works at one of the events at the Hong Kong Literary Festival 2012, organized to introduce emerging writers to the public. These are some of the tangible outcomes – those that I know of – of the creative writing course I have been teaching at my current institution. The future of English language literary scene in Hong Kong depends on the linguistic landscape in as much as it depends on the ecology of writers, editors, publishers and institutions that are supportive of the writing arts. Creative writing as a form of cultural critique is able to facilitate the formation of dual beings who are participating in the future of the imagined community that is Hong Kong. This imagined community, I argue, is a testimony to the biophily that would shape or perhaps even exceed legal, political and constitutional definitions of the territory. This, then, is the importance of bringing society into the classroom.

TEACHING ARTHUR YAP'S POEMS

How may we teach the works of a poet in such a way as to bring society into the classroom? The personae in Arthur Yap's poetry are often standing still, immobilized and moved to contemplation. The often-unnamed settings in his poems frequently receive a second or third mental visitation, as if to invite us to explore the treatment of the spaces and places of his poetry.

I remember first encountering Arthur Yap's poetry alongside those of Edwin Thumboo's and Lee Tzu Pheng's as an undergraduate at the National University of Singapore. I recall being frustrated by Yap's poems, for unlike Thumboo's "Ulysses by the Merlion" which cements the relationship between poetry and nation building and Lee's "My Country and My People" which is wary of being co-opted by the nation building discourse, Yap's poems seem not to want to say anything in this regard. Yap's poems read frequently like arrested departures; they are often negations of the past without the promise of a movement into the present or future. I was frustrated by the fact that much of his poems are solipsistic and that they represent a resignation from everyday reality, not unlike the Zen garden celebrated in his poem "The Shisen-Do":

> always the same tableau, intrinsically still,
> the kindling of every sentience,
> it is always the same & one can see
> it has always been, will be. (Yap *Man Snake Apple* 33)

Rightly or wrongly, that was the impression that remained with me with regards to Yap's poetry.

Previously at the University of Hong Kong and currently at the Chinese University of Hong Kong where I am now based, I have taught at various times the poems of Thumboo, Lee and those of Alfian Sa'at's in an undergraduate introductory course on poetry that culminates in a reading of the urban Anglophone poetry of contemporary Singapore, Hong Kong and Malaysia. I include Alfian's poems in the course because his is a voice that represents a development in Singapore poetry in so far as it is one that is publicly and explicitly anti-establishment. His unruly voice is especially significant since Singapore's development as a nation has been premised on state control with the acquiescence of its citizens. However, I have consciously avoided teaching Yap's poems, for they seem not to want to say anything about the society and culture of Singapore. For what is one to do with poems such as "Paired Stills" in *Man Snake Apple*, a poem which celebrates the way language is able to present a series of tableaux unadorned with any social and cultural commentary whatsoever?

I have the suspicion that I have yet to learn how to appreciate his poems in order to teach them in such a way as to explore the various aspects of Singapore society. Much of my frustration has to do with the two main features of his poetry. First, solipsism is the main characteristic and theme of his poetry. In poems such as "Street Scene II", we are witness to a "solipsist's nightmare" in which the external world diminishes the self, to the point where the self is annihilated and becomes "a big foeval eye" (Yap *Man Snake Apple* 24). Second, the poems tend to revel in word-play and keep external reality at bay. Prominent examples include "the grammar of a dinner" and "a lesson on the definite article" in *Down the Line*. To give another example: in "Paraphrase", a journey is contained within language, to the extent that "the word swallows the world/ [and] the word comes close to carrying its own ontology" (Yap *Man Snake Apple* 31). It is as if the poems refrain from engaging with the socially-shared world among people. The features of Yap's poems are such that Rajeev Patke has observed that they possess "the riddling solipsism of one who would rather talk to himself" (94).

Yap's poems may be usefully read alongside those of Charles Baudelaire's in that their poems present "the gaze of the alienated man" (Benjamin *Writer of Modern Life* 40). Baudelaire's personae adopt the role of the *flâneur*, both as the disinterested observer as well as participant of street scenes in Paris. Yap's personae, in contrast, are often immobilized by street scenes. Time and again, in poems such as "late-night bonus" in *Down the Line* as well as "Street Scene I" in *Man Snake Apple*, Yap's personae withdraw from engagement with what he sees and hears and shun human contact. Walter Benjamin has made the point that Baudelaire "placed shock experience…at the very center of his art" (*Writer of Modern Life* 178). In contrast, Yap's poetry is the very inverse of Baudelaire's in that much of it recedes into language and away from sense impressions, so that the shock of reality is deferred for as long as possible. If an engagement with the external world is presented as a nightmarish proposition for the solipsist as in the case of "Street Scene II", and if Yap's poetry wishes for language to carry its own ontology as in the case of "Paraphrase", such that it cannot bear the weight of a reality that is external to language, then to what extent can one say that what is presented in Yap's poetry is actually saying something about the society of Singapore?

Patke argues that "the poet in Singapore bears an over-determined relation to the development of the state into nation, especially during the first few decades of the history of poetry in Singapore" (90). This is especially so, given Singapore's rapid development from colony to modern nation state (90). Patke's point is that the voices of the poets in Singapore have been arbitrarily split into the private and the public, and both sides of this dichotomy rely on the fossilized relationships between the poets, the state, and the nation, relationships that have been taken for granted in the writing of poetry (96). (One wonders if the same may be said of my pedagogical approach to the poetry of Singapore, in that it has an over-determined relation to the development of the state into nation.) If I find the poems of Alfian, Thumboo and Lee easy to teach, it is because they can be easily read as being explicit in terms of their relationship to the state and to the nation building project. Alfian's poems can be read as having a public voice that resists the intrusion of the state. Thumboo's poems can be read as having a public voice aligned with nation building. In turn, Lee's poems can be read as having a private voice that is wary about making public pronouncements about the state and nation building.

The poems of Yap, on the other hand, often forestall this arbitrary dichotomy between the public and the private because they are so reflexive. "In the Quiet of the Night" in *Man Snake Apple* is a poem about the act of reading poetry; it situates the act of reading as switching back and forth between the public and the private and between contrastive states of understanding and ignorance (17). The poem is content to move back and forth between opposing states, hence forestalling attempts at meaning-making and signification. Furthermore, many of them are often meta-poetic in character. His poems draw attention to themselves as artifices before entering into the process of signification. Consider the following from "Still-Life II" which is a comment on the act of writing:

> i think everything's comical,
> as comical as anything that isn't
> in this arrangement:
>
> this rite of writing
> which doesn't provide an option
> to any other kind of mindedness.
>
> it is very clear
> this scribble has no ambiguity
> because you haven't. (Yap *Man Snake Apple* 4)

To the solipsist, everything external to the poem is comical; eventually, so is everything within the poem. The poem demonstrates the process by which a poem which is an artifice enters into meaning. It acknowledges that we are meaning-making beings that cannot tolerate ambiguity. Even as it seeks to establish a linguistic enclosure with its own ontology, it fails to do so. The solipsism is dismantled. The poem *must* have a persona. It has an "I" for other people. The poem *must* mean something for others. The poem lacks ambiguity because it has a reader who refuses to grant it to the poem. A poem such as this reminds me of the final moment in Samuel Beckett's *The Unnamable*, where there is a struggle both against and for meaning – "in the silence you don't know, you must go on, I can't go on, I'll go on" (476).

If I have devoted some time to draw attention to the solipsistic nature of Yap's poetry, to its reflexivity and to its preoccupation with linguistic play, it is because these are the aspects and thematic concerns of his poetry that I have to acknowledge and work through before I can read and understand the poems' engagement with social reality. It has to be said that the "poetics of the nation" in Yap's poetry as examined by Robbie B. H. Goh in "Imagining the Nation: The Role of Singapore Poetry in English in 'Emergent Nationalism'" is first and foremost a poetics that is reflexive and conscious of itself as a linguistic artifact (26). For unlike most of the poems of Thumboo, Alfian and Lee, those of Yap remind us again and again that poetry is, first and foremost, an artifice forged out of language. This is the kind of reading I believe I have to perform so as to do justice to Yap's poetry before I am able to teach them to undergraduates.

How then may one begin to teach the reading of place and space within Yap's poetry? We must learn to trace a path out of the solipsism of Yap's poetry and indeed, his poems often leave an opening out of the solipsism, as indicated in the poem "Paraphrase", whereby it is acknowledged that "the word comes close to carrying its own ontology" (Yap *Man Snake Apple* 31). Language is *almost* granted its own ontology, almost but not quite. If his "scribble has no ambiguity", it is by virtue of the fact that we as teachers and readers have to strip it of its ambiguity (Yap *Man Snake Apple* 4). We have to be stubborn readers who read against the grain, who refuse to "provide an option / to any other kind of mindedness" (Yap *Man Snake Apple* 4).

Here, I invoke Michel de Certeau's playful characterization of reading, in that the text is a site for "advances and retreats, tactics and games" (175). De Certeau's invoking of Claude Lévi-Strauss's analysis of *bricolage* is useful in this context (174). As a teacher and as a reader, I play the artless *bricoleur*. I am interested in improvising and making do with "the materials at hand", materials that were originally fashioned for other uses in other contexts (de Certeau 174). Hence, to understand the treatment of spaces and places within Yap's poetry, I propose that we appeal to basic concepts in cultural geography as well as ecocriticism so as to explore how these concepts pertain to spaces and places in Singapore as mediated through the poems.

As this is a course that seeks to introduce basic concepts of cultural geography to enhance our reading of Yap's poetry, I feel that it is important for us to be grounded in the concepts of urban and cultural geography as outlined in introductory books such as *Key Concepts in Urban Geography* and *Key Concepts in Geography*. Cultural geography, broadly speaking for our purposes here, is the study of the relationships between cultural processes/conventions/commodities and spaces/places, and there is an aspect of geography that pertains to the study of literature. As Alison Blunt points out, "[g]eographers have increasingly turned their attention not only to 'writing' and the 'world' being written about, but also to the wider politics and poetics of representation" (68). As she observes, "[o]ne key theme has been an attempt to explore geographies of writing in both imaginative and material contexts and in the very form of writing itself" (Blunt 70). As such, I find it useful to direct undergraduates to concepts such as place, space, public space, public housing, and so on, as a way of entering into an exploration of Yap's poetry.

Perhaps the first concept to introduce to the undergraduates is that of space. As Nigel Thrift notes, geographers have "abandon[ed] the idea of any pre-existing space in which things are passively embedded…for an idea of space as [that which is] undergoing continual construction as a result of the agency of things encountering each other in more or less organized circulations" (86). As such, space is not viewed simply as a vacuum in which people and objects inhabit, but rather, as a dynamic construct that is transformed by its negotiation with people as well as social and cultural processes, norms and objects. Closely related to the notion of space is that of place, which "consists of particular rhythms of being that confirm and naturalize the existence of certain spaces" (Thrift 92). A place is a space that is internalized in the minds of people as to possess certain meanings and purposes. Place "is involved with embodiment", and this means that a place has an effect on the behavior of those within it (Thrift 92). One would behave differently in a wet market as opposed to when one is in a public library, partly because these different places have different functions and possess different codes of behavior. When we look at Yap's poetry with these concepts in mind, we realize that many of his poems map out for us micro-processes whereby space and places influence the behavior and norms of its inhabitants.

An understanding of Yap's poetics of emplacement may begin with the treatment of public space in his poetry. The word "space" in the phrase "public space" has more than one meaning. On the one hand, it may refer to the "space used in common by the public", such as parks and playgrounds; on the other hand, it may "refer to the spaces that are owned and controlled by the state", such as government and parliamentary offices (Latham et. al. 177). In view of this, on the one hand, the term "public" may simply mean a collection of private individuals; on the other hand, it may imply "a notion of the public as being conceptually homologous with the state and its citizens", hence drawing attention to the contract between the state and its people (Latham et. al. 177). It is important to highlight the fact that Singapore is an island-nation-state, and much of its spaces are compressed within a relatively small land area. Hence, there is a need for efficient management and regulation of land so as to meet the demands of economic growth without compromising the standard of living of its inhabitants. In Yap's poems, we find an articulation of this condition, to the extent that public spaces in Singapore are portrayed to be organizing and regulating the behavior and norms of society.

The poem "dramatis personae" is a critique of the concept of the public that operates in public spaces. The flowers in a park are not meant to be picked, because "they are for the public", whereas "we in public are private figures" (Yap *Down the Line* 6). As the poem demonstrates, the notion of the public that operates within a public space such as the park is a disciplinary logic that regulates the private individual. The poem draws attention to the notion that it is space that regulates us, or, to put it in another way, we are circumscribed by our spaces, for "we would never have been / more than all these things we have seen" (Yap *Down the Line* 7). There is a hint of eco-criticism at work in this poem, for there is a suggestion that the polluted beach portrayed in this tableau, created by human neglect, in turn circumscribes our vision of who we are.

If public spaces operate with a disciplinary logic, then what about *public housing*? In Singapore, approximately eighty-five per cent of the land allocated for residential purposes is developed by the state and provided for as public housing by the Housing and Development Board (HDB), Singapore's public housing authority. Public housing, especially within the context of Singapore, represents the ambivalent nature of what constitutes public and private space. On the one hand, they are private spaces as they are familial and personal sites; on the other hand, they represent contracts on the part of citizens with the state. That these HDB flats are sold on a 99-year leasehold basis further complicates the notion of ownership and hence complicates the dichotomy between what is public and private, and between what is public and private ownership.

The ubiquitous nature of HDB public housing in Singapore's physical landscape is testimony to the extent to which the state is able to intervene in the everyday life of Singaporeans. Chua Beng Huat in his aptly titled article "Public Housing Residents as Clients of the State" has made the point that the state is the "monopoly supplier of housing for the nation" (51). He points out that in the 1960s, the public housing program "was initially met with resistance from residents affected by resettlement"; however, "by the mid-1970s, such resistance had dissipated" ("Public Housing Residents" 47). As Chua argues, the "successful provision of public housing and concomitant improvement of the material conditions of Singaporeans have paid great political dividend" in terms of securing the allegiance of Singaporeans to the state ("Public Housing Residents" 48). Hence, HDB flats are a testimony to the legitimacy of the state; they also signify the state's power in fostering a culture that is concerned with upward social mobility that is aligned with capitalist values.

Yap's poems demonstrate this collusion between the space of public housing and material acquisition, competition and education (which is seen as a guarantor of upward social mobility). "2 mothers in a hdb playground" in *Down the Line* presents two mothers engaged in verbal one-upmanship, each extolling the academic abilities of their children as well as their material extravagance (Yap 54-55). In "i think (a book of changes)", the story of Singapore's economic development is told from the point of view of someone who views moving into a high-rise flat as a sign of financial and material attainment (Yap *Down the Line* 53). In "samson & delilah", other parents are portrayed as being concerned over the image of their neighborhood as a result of a boy's unkempt appearance and pre-occupation with rock music (Yap *Down the Line* 20). While "samson & delilah" may not explicitly set its narrative within a HDB flat, the prevailing sense of claustrophobia, social intimacy, as well as the concern over how one is perceived by one's neighbors and friends suggest a community of high-rise dwellers. Given that Yap's *Down the Line* was published in 1980, his poems may be said to anticipate the work of Alfian Sa'at, whose poems "Void Deck" and "Jobweek 1992" in his 1998 collection *One Fierce Hour* develop further the critique of everyday life in HDB flats.

In other poems, Yap maps out for us in minutiae the consequences of living and working within urban space. Built-up areas of high human density are regularly portrayed as sites of disenchantment and apathy in Yap's poetry. As Yap puts it in the poem "down the line", there is "a habit by which the world moves, [whereby] people will not /look at the centre of things" (Yap *Down the Line* 10). In more than one poem, Yap demonstrates a pre-occupation with suicide and society's apathy towards such incidents. Hence, in the poem "statement", a person's declared intention of suicide is regarded with indifference in the office: "so if you say: please may I jump/ off the ledge? & go on to add/ this work is really killing,/you will be told: start jumping" (Yap *Down the Line* 5). Likewise, in "down the line":

we say that a person who had stabbed himself
19 times & then thrown his own body over
the balcony is unbelievable reportage.
if you tell me times enough, tired, i will believe
or, at least, agree. & if you tell me
times more, angered, i will throw
the narrated body back at you (*Down the Line* 9)

Again, in "10th floor Song":

no need to bring the ambulance
to the porch
(whoever she was)
left leg over first floor ledge
was quite dead. (*Only Lines* 25)

Insofar as balconies and ledges form the backdrop to actions and intentions, the logic of urban space is a logic that is inhuman, "for its basis well under the skin has yet another/ lined in rubrics" (Yap *Down the Line* 9). Urban space is presented in Yap's poems as a totality that consumes its inhabitants, to the point that any articulation of the human is futile: "if tomorrow someone sings a confessional/ of some 'ism or other, the refrain sinks in/ as only a totality & any event, being given,/ predetermined, is at the onset already silent" (Yap *Down the Line* 9). Likewise, in "topnote", urban space is presented as a "superordinate thing", to the extent that it overrides human agency (Yap *Down the Line* 25). Given the pessimism of Yap's poetry, it is easy to see why his poems refuse to bear much reality and tend to remain within language, as in the case of the poem "Paraphrase" mentioned earlier.

If the logic of urban space is such that it absorbs human impulses into its own totality, then it is no wonder that Yap's poems portray the development of urban space with some measure of anxiety and resignation. Take the often-studied poem "old house at ang siang hill" for example – we are told that the addressee's personal past in the house is "superannuated grime" (Yap *Only Lines* 21). The house may have been an "unusual house" because it holds special memories for certain individuals or perhaps because it represents "straits-born" (Peranakan) tastes and culture in terms of its furnishings. Yet this does not prevent the house from being demolished (Yap *Only Lines* 21). The persona in the poem is articulating the urban logic to which the eradication of "this house-that-was" is a necessity in the name of progress (Yap *Only Lines* 21). In the end, there will be no sign that the house (and the culture it represents) once existed and "nothing much will be missed" (Yap *Only Lines* 21). Yap's other frequently-discussed poem "there is no future in nostalgia" likewise displays a measure of resignation, not as much pertaining to the loss of cultural memory but to the loss of human presence. The "corner cigarette-seller" is "replaced by a stamp-machine", "the old cook by a pressure-cooker" and "the old trishaw-rider's stand by a fire hydrant" (Yap *Commonplace* 39). What is particularly disturbing, of course, is that human roles are replaced with utilitarian material objects, and this is an inevitable condition in the name of "progress".

It is clear that much of Yap's poetry has to do with dwelling (or rather, the lack thereof). Dwelling, a concept drawn from the field of ecocriticism, has to do with "practical existence as an immediate reality", "a relation of duty and responsibility" as well as "the long-term imbrication of humans in a landscape of memory, ancestry and death, of ritual, life and work" (Garrard 108). In much of Yap's poetry, and as already anticipated by the earlier discussion of "old house at ang siang hill", we are witnesses to the failure at dwelling. In "late-night bonus", the unruly behavior of teenagers at night is something "every street has known" (Yap *Down the Line* 43), just as in "sights", urban spaces are arranged and packaged for tourism rather than for its inhabitants: "the sights are like every city's offerings./ the difference is that, here, it is possible/ to combine country & sea, a lovely/ bilocation for the economy tourist" (Yap *Down the Line* 46). Perhaps the poems may be suggesting that much of this failure at dwelling has to do with the pathological relationship of inhabitants towards their environment. In "nature study", nature is presented as being subject to instrumentalization: "the tree moaned in a series of multiple snaps", and a tree trunk is now ironically a wooden "frame around the picture / of trees & idyllic nature" (Yap *Down the Line* 41). In "old tricks for new houses", the process of land reclamation to build residential areas is commented on sardonically ("your neighbours will hang crabshells / on their pomegranate plants as saline testimony"), indicating the kind of one-sided relationship that exists between the environment and its unmindful inhabitants (Yap Down the Line 26). There is a split between the realm of the human and the environment. The environment here is shown to be something inert, to be acted upon, shaped and manipulated. While it cannot be said that Yap's poems constitute an explicit and elaborate ecocritical agency, it cannot be denied nonetheless that there is an ecocritical aspect to his poetics.

From our reading of the various poems, a portrait of the relationship between space and human agency begins to emerge. On the one hand, urban space connotes economic and material advancement; on the other hand, the price of these is the rapid alienation of people from the environment and from themselves. There is, as demonstrated in the poems "old house at ang siang hill" and "there is no future in nostalgia", the loss and eradication of memory, meaning and culture even as urban spaces are being developed (and re-developed) in the name of social-economic progress. The promise of material and economic advancement is negated by scenes of stasis, immobility and alienation. Poems after poems, we witness organized spaces and places that are inhospitable to human agency. There is an irony in the heart of Yap's poetry, in that social-economic progress as permeated through spaces results in the loss of the social and personal. Yap's poetry may be said to be offering us a critique of the society and culture of Singapore through its portrayal of places and spaces. In respect, the writings of Henri Lefebvre are helpful in directing us towards the critical possibilities of Yap's poetry.

DWELLING

This section overlays our discussions in the previous section with philosophical discussions of the notion of space. It weaves the insights offered by Lefebvre's *The Production of Space* into our reading of Yap's poetry. As we shall see, the Heideggerian and neo-Marxist influences in Lefebvre's writings are useful because they enable us to move towards an understanding of Yap's critique of spatial practices in Singapore.

Three concepts pertaining to space – what Lefebvre calls "the triad of the perceived, the conceived, and the lived" – form the underlying structure to Lefebvre's *Production of Space* (39). Perceived space leads to the creation of "spatial practice", which has to do with people's understanding of physical and concrete places (Lefebvre 38). Spatial practices structure a person's behavior and routines which in turn engender the wholeness and durability of a society. Conceived space, or "representations of space", is "conceptualized space, the space of scientists, planners, urbanists, technocratic subdividers and social engineers...all of whom identify what is lived and what is perceived with what is conceived" (Lefebvre 38). In other words, conceived space is the product of mental abstraction, of the political and rational-instrumental impulse. It is executed through state-planning, blueprints and technology. Lived spaces, that which is experienced in our everyday lives, are "representational spaces" (39). They evoke collective or personal emotional associations and are invested with meanings. They are the space of social relations, of recognition and action. A church, a post office and a house are examples of lived spaces.

Lefebvre's *The Production of Space*, as Stuart Elden reminds us, "should be read between Marx and Heidegger" (189). Marx, because Lefebvre is interested in critiquing space as a function of capitalism, arguing that we are alienated from ourselves because of the conceived spaces we are used to inhabiting. Heidegger, because spaces and places, insofar as they are something felt, lived, and experienced, come under the rubric of phenomenology. What emerges from Lefebvre's book is the insight that, given the statist/capitalist mode of production, it is conceived space, the space which is the product of mental abstraction, which colonizes lived and perceived space.

Yap's poetry converges with Lefebvre's insight as it presents us with spaces and places that are overwritten with state power. We see in Yap's poetry the product of conceived space, the space of technocrats, politicians, and urban planners. The ending of "old house at ang siang hill", for instance, testifies to the eradication of lived places by conceived places: "nothing much will be missed / eyes not tradition tell you this" (*Only Lines* 21). In the end, one's memory of lived spaces is overwritten by the materiality of conceived spaces. As Lefebvre argues, the "modern state promotes and imposes itself as the stable centre", and this is manifested in its administration of space (23). Urban spaces, as portrayed in Yap's writings, are revealed to be conceptualized around a rational-instrumentalist logic such that it has "rearranged/ the calefaction of the thermometer/ we regulate by" (Yap *Down the Line* 11).

Often, the tone of Yap's poetry takes on a tinge of disaffection and cynicism. The voice is often sardonic, as in the case of "down the line", a poem that speaks of disenchantment with conceived space which is the space of management, regulation and control: "the wind that weaves across buildings/ carries the calculus the city is reckoned on" (Yap *Down the Line* 9). What is conspicuous in the poem "down the line" is the absence of life, of dwelling, of the human; it is a poem portraying a dystopia, a community of automatons: "what everyone will tell you is what everyone/ wants to hear, has been told" (Yap *Down the Line* 11).

As such, a reading of Yap's poetry would quickly reveal that the poems are testimony to the exhaustion of the psyche and imagination. Many of Yap's poems speak of exhaustion and disappointment. In "Still-Life V", a persona speaks of the gap that exists between the self and one's environment, be it a library or park: "where does rigour end & rigor mortis begin?/ so slender is the distinction, & practice/ ensures the perfection of numbing the sensibilities" (*Man Snake Apple* 7). There is a suggestion here that, despite the technical mastery over one's environment, there is a gap between the external landscape and the human.

Such conceived spaces are accompanied by diminished social life. Lefebvre, in a Marxist moment in his book, argues that "[i]f reality is taken in the sense of materiality, social reality no longer *has* reality, nor *is* it reality" [emphases in original] (81). Everything has to be placed within a circuit of "money, commodities, and the exchange of material goods", to the extent that one person's interest in another does not exist outside of this circuit (Lefebvre 81). Yap's poetry articulates this insight as in the case of "Street-Scene I", whereby an encounter between two strangers demonstrates the loneliness of urban experience:

i think he didn't want to ask anything
except: why am i so lonely & have to stop you?
i felt the same then, as he walked on,
he seemed to grow larger & larger,
ignoring the laws of perspective   (*Man Snake Apple* 23)

If the physical enlargement of the figure of loneliness finds articulation here as a conceit against the laws of perspective, it is because there is no provision within the realm of the material for the presentation of the loss of the social. This loss of the social is presented even more poignantly in "Still-Life IV", a poem about a gathering of friends. In the poem, the gathering of friends is presented as a non-event, to the effect that even their children are immobilized, knowingly impassive and insensible: "they have no demands/ to make of anyone. they have nothing to remember/ or to forget. they know exactly what is, isn't,/ going to happen next" (*Man Snake Apple* 6). The conversation is of no consequence, and material objects such as cups, plates and the table form the center of the scene, as if implying that only the material is of consequence. Yap's poetry overlays a disquieting poetic and emotional geography over the material space of Singapore. Hence, it is not surprising that the emotional quality of many of the poems is that of resignation.

It is no wonder then that Yap's poetry is preoccupied with solipsism. It is as if to suggest that the material urban space (and the objects in it) is a space inadequate to a poetics that seeks to engage with social reality. In this respect, Yap engages with the very same concerns Heidegger explores in his essay "Building Dwelling Thinking", in which the latter explores the issue of dwelling and its relationship with physical buildings. For Heidegger, dwelling is not the same as residing within a building or house: "today's houses may even be well planned, easy to keep, attractively cheap, open to air, light, and sun, but – do the houses in themselves hold any guarantee that dwelling occurs in them?" [emphasis in original] (146). Rather, *dwelling* has to do with one's sense of self and one's place in the world. "Still-Life VII" may be regarded as a rejoinder to Heidegger's question:

a house, i know, is but a temporary abode
but how satisfying to find one which harmonizes:
curtain ears close to the ground,
the forehead slopes towards glasspanes
& holds up a nose, a plant in a beige pot
spreading little moist sibilances in the rain.

two big arms run a path in the garden,
draw up sparrows, dun squirrels, still as stone
near columns of grass, green as spring tea. (*Man Snake Apple* 9)

The poem portrays the house as an embodiment of the self: it is "habitual" in the Heideggerian sense that one is able to inhabit a building or home (147). What Heidegger calls dwelling is presented as harmony in Yap's poetry, whereby one's abode is symmetrical to the self. This poem serves as a reminder of what has been lost to Singapore's urban landscape, as portrayed in some many of Yap's other poems: our capacity to dwell.

Our conventional thinking about dwelling, as Heidegger informs us, is analogous to our conventional thinking about language: "Man acts as though *he* were the shaper and master of language, while in fact *language* remains the master of man" [emphases in original] (146). Language exists before we were born, and our acquisition of language is akin to finding a place within the symbolic domain already in existence. Likewise, to dwell is to recognize one's place within a pre-existing space. But if this pre-existing space is a conceived space in the Lefebvrian sense, in the sense that it has already been overwritten by technocrats, politicians, and urban planners, then the notion of dwelling has to be revised. For if we continue with the analogy of space with language, then that which is homologous to Lefebvre's notion of conceived space is something like Newspeak in George Orwell's novel *1984*. This explains why so many of the poems we have seen are testimonies to failure at dwelling. The home is often the space of intrusion, as in the case of "old house at ang siang hill" which, as we have previously discussed, is a poem about the eradication of a much-cherished and personal interiority in the name of progress.

If Yap's poetry is preoccupied with solipsism, it is because for the solipsist, urban space is a space that is already compromised. Dwelling for the solipsist is possible only when interiority is reduced to the self. That is why Yap's poetics are so different to those of Thumboo's and Alfian's. Thumboo's often-discussed "Ulysses by the Merlion" addresses itself mostly to conceived spaces, spaces of national commemoration. Its attempt at conferring a mythic status onto the Merlion is compromised right from the beginning by the Merlion's ubiquity as a commoditized tourist icon. Alfian's poems, in contrast, are able to present conceived spaces as imbued with "[a] sense of things reduced" and hence as "place[s] to be avoided", even though they do not comment on the impossibility of avoiding conceived spaces (4).

Yap's poetry is not an easy read. Very often, the poems tend to fold into themselves and elude attempts at meaning-making. Nonetheless, what gradually emerges from our reading of Yap is an urban poetics that seeks refuge in solipsism because urban space has been overwritten by the state. What is a poet to do in response to the state dominance of urban space? For Yap, the answer is to be "a big foeval eye", to fold into the self and be constantly vigilant, looking outwards (Yap *Man Snake Apple* 24).

THE POETICS OF THE UMBRELLA MOVEMENT

We need to be vigilant just as we need to keep vigil over the streets. At the end of 2014, for about 2-3 months, the whole of Hong Kong was concerned with Occupy Central. "Occupy Central" was, and still is, a loaded term and event which represents many different things to many different people. The normative take on it would be that it was a political movement first initiated by 3 people, which was then overtaken by student organizations and independent volunteer groups. It was a political campaign for genuine universal suffrage first proposed by Benny Tai, a law professor at the University of Hong Kong, Chan Kin-man, a sociology professor at my university, the Chinese University of Hong Kong, and Chu Yiu-ming, a human rights activist and a clergyman. The original plans to occupy Admiralty for a few days were quickly exceeded by the occupation of 2 additional sites, Mong Kok and Causeway Bay for 79 days.

You could say that the original organizers of Occupy Central became supporters of the Umbrella Movement. That the original plans for Occupy Central were exceeded and extended in such a decentralized manner is instructive, and you could see that for some of the protesters, it meant questioning a certain way of life under the regime of capitalism known as Hong Kong. Occupy Central, or the Umbrella Movement, if you prefer the term, was that overflow of social, political, and aesthetic desire that was the object of endless debate at newspaper and TV forums, dinner tables and in street scuffles.

The activities and symbolic objects at the three sites underscored the relationship between political protest and art-making. The Umbrella Movement represented an outbreak of vernacular symbolic expressions in search of an imagined community it was already establishing. I would argue that the protest sites were both material and symbolic, inviting a public to imagine a Hong Kong nationhood, even as such an act was fraught with anxieties, conflicts and tensions. For the Umbrella Movement was an event that was yet to come; now, it is entirely feasible that it will be an event that is always already present, even if had ended as a material event.

The above photograph shows chalk graffiti on the pavement at the Admiralty site. It was a beautiful work of art, and for some reason the colors (though not evident in the monochrome image here) were actually very luminous. The artwork was temporary because of its nature, and of course it no longer exists, at least not physically. Or you could say it now exists in the form of photographs. The point I am trying to make is that the Umbrella Movement existed not only as material objects or as physical sites, but also as lived experience and memory. I am trying, though the use of street photography, to take us through some of these lived moments

I am inspired by Michel Foucault, who uses this term "history of the present" to describe his work in *Discipline and Punish*:

> I would like to write the history of this prison, with all the political investments of the body that it gathers together in its closed architecture. Why? Simply because I am interested in the past? No, if one means by that writing a history of the past in terms of the present. Yes, if one means writing a history of the present. (30-31)

One of the high points in Foucault's *Discipline and Punish* has to do with his analysis of panopticism. The Panopticon, as we have learnt from Foucault's history of the prison, is also at work in modern societies, reminding us constantly of the need to discipline ourselves in institutional sites within which we are located. I am hoping to find in some of the images we are going to see certain moments that speak to us about us. "Writing a history of the present", as Michael S. Roth points out, "means writing a history *in* the present; self-consciously writing in a field of power relations and political struggle." (43) A history of the present is a self-conscious writing of the present, and I am conscious of the methods that are available to me even as I was writing this. As a Singaporean who has lived in Hong Kong for more than a decade, I think of myself as an outsider on the inside. What could I know of the Umbrella Movement, given my background as a street photographer, a poet and a student of literature?

I am very much interested in thick description so as to sketch out the Umbrella Movement that I know, ever mindful of Clifford Geertz's warning that "(t)he danger that cultural analysis...will lose touch with the hard surfaces of life... is an ever-present one" (30). Just as Foucault's notion of the Panopticon, drawn from his study of the prison, has become a powerful critical notion that shows us how things work in modern institutions, I am interested in looking at various moments, objects and scenes of the Umbrella Movement so as to begin to think about what the protest movement means to Hong Kong.

On 22nd September 2014, the first day of the student boycott at the Chinese University of Hong Kong and a week before Occupy Central was planned to commence, I walked around with two to three film and digital cameras, trying to capture various scenes as they begin to speak to me.

The previous two photographs were taken on that day and represent the self-reflexivity involved in my project. Even at the time, I knew I was not the only person responding to the Umbrella Movement through art. These are photographs in the act of catching a painter in the act of sketching out the scene of the student boycott at my university.

I have not had the chance to confirm this, but unless I am mistaken, the painter is Perry Dino. As reported in the *South China Morning Post*, he specializes in painting street protests (Carney "Perry Dino"). Here, he is using street art (as opposed to "studio art") to engage with and commemorate political events.

I remember feeling somewhat annoyed at the person on the left whose umbrella was blocking my view, the result of which was that I had to maneuver a bit to get a shot of the entire canvas but without the actual scene depicted on it. A lot has been said about how the umbrella is a literal and symbolic object of political and material expediency of the Hong Kong people, sheltering them from the sun, rain and pepper spray. But if you take this symbol seriously, one might say that from the point of view of the protesters, the Hong Kong government has not been a good enough umbrella to them. This is why they needed to create their own.

This image is of the site-specific art installation known as the Umbrella Patchwork, created by students from the Academy of Visual Arts at Hong Kong Baptist University ("Umbrella Patchwork"). It was made out of the canopies of about 200-250 broken umbrellas that belonged to protesters who were defending themselves from pepper spray and teargas on the night of 28th September. The Chinese character on the balloon is "chang", meaning "to support", or "to hold something up". The students were holding up the pepper spray and teargas-stained umbrellas, in full view of those working in the government offices nearby.

To extend the umbrella motif, you could say that, from the point of view of the protesters, because the Hong Kong government could not be that secure umbrella to its people, local residents would have had to fashion their own, and these were the broken umbrellas and poor living conditions the students held up for display.

This, then, was the imagined community of Hong Kong, with an imagined leader. This cutout of an ironically photoshopped image showing the Chinese President Xi Jinping as an umbrella totting protestor was a popular and potent symbol for the movement. Here was a protest movement that knew it was being watched, that was producing accessible symbols legible to the world at large. To have lived in tents was to have lived in that imagined community, to proclaim a state of homelessness, to protest the high rent and property prices that were (and still are) out of reach to the average Hong Kong person. It was a protest against having to resort to living in subdivided flats and cage homes.

The Umbrella Movement took place against a backdrop of the high profile corruption court case in which Rafael Hui, the former Chief Secretary of the Hong Kong Administration (the city's second highest government post) and property developer Thomas Kwok were charged and found guilty of corruption. C.Y. Leung, the then-Chief Executive was himself mired in a scandal involving a secret $7 million payout from an Australian engineering company UGL while in public office.

Leung, of course, used to be a big player himself in the property business. As reported in the *New York Times*, he has commented on how genuine democracy is not possible because "then obviously you would be talking to half of the people in Hong Kong who earn less than [US] $1,800 a month" (Bradsher "Hong Kong Leader Affirms Unbending Stance"). Given this, the allusion to George Orwell's *Animal Farm* is especially poignant. Again, as you can see, this was a movement that knew it was being watched, and was very shrewd with its use of very accessible allusions.

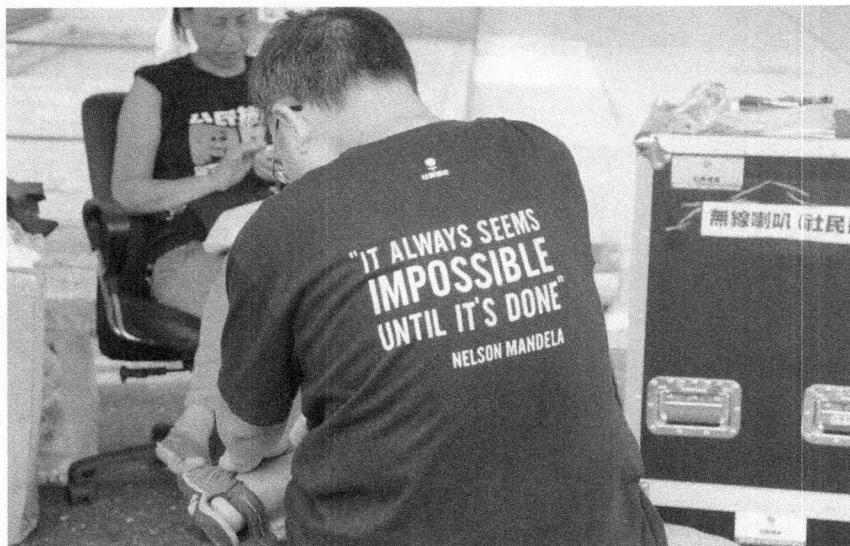

The Umbrella Movement was to a large extent a work of bricolage, patching together various moments from history, literature and pop culture, drawing its power from various movements and impulses from various times.

The quote by Nelson Mandela on the man's shirt refers to the anti-apartheid movement in South Africa; the poem on the banner is "My Generation" by Gu Cheng (顧城) and roughly translates as "The dark night gave me dark eyes, but I'm using them to look for brightness". Gu Cheng was one of the "Misty Poets" (朦胧诗人) exiled after the Tiananmen crackdown of 1989 – that's another

allusion there. John Lennon, of course, stands for the anti-Vietnam War protests and 1960s counter culture. At various times, you could hear the soundtrack of "Can You Hear the People Sing" blaring from speakers at Admiralty. This was from the musical *Les Misérables* which in turn was adapted from Victor Hugo's novel which alludes to the Paris Uprising of 1832.

The protest had its semiotic roots in populism, mass participation and even touristic spectatorship. If you were an historian, you would probably try to measure up the various historical moments with one another and of course, acknowledge these are all disparate and very contingent events in history. Yet the references were meant to be quickly grasped by a lay public, and no lengthy explications were necessary for the references to do their work. This was a very culturally shrewd protest that utilized pop culture and literary and historical references for its cause.

The Lennon Wall was a work of participatory art, making use of the very act of popular participation as political strength. It was inspired by the Lennon Wall in Prague, on which political dissidents used the lyrics of John Lennon and the Beatles to protest the former Communist regime. Perhaps the Umbrella Movement was enacting its own version of the 1989 Velvet Revolution, which had brought about a peaceful end to Communism in what was then Czechoslovakia. Hong Kong in 2014 was looking back at 1989 Czechoslovakia, re-imagining or dreaming a new country into existence. I am not an historian, so this might be a rather tenuous and blunt statement: but perhaps the 1989 Velvet Revolution may be seen as the successful counterpart to the 1989 Tiananmen protest.

You may say that I am a dreamer, but perhaps the wall is that dream of what might have been. At the Lennon Wall in Hong Kong, the public posted their dreams and hopes, as a protest both against the Communist regime in China and the excesses of Hong Kong's capitalist regime.

The protest movement was rhizomatic in nature, in that although it was first proposed by the 3 founders of Occupy Central, it was taken over by two student groups. Scholarism was led by Joshua Wong who appeared on the cover of the Asian edition of Time Magazine, and the Hong Kong Federation of Students was led by Alex Chow its secretary-general and Lester Shum its vice secretary. These are all very young people between 18-22 years of age and I was amazed by their energy and commitment.

I would like to invoke Gilles Deleuze and Félix Guattari's notion of the rhizome here to describe the Umbrella Movement. The rhizomatic conception of knowledge is a departure from the binary understanding of this versus that, causes vs effects. Rather, it invites us to see knowledge and events as having multiple courses and intersections, and multiple beginnings and end-points.

As Deleuze and Guattari tell us in *A Thousand Plateaus*, "A rhizome ceaselessly establishes connections between semiotic chains, organizations of power, and circumstances relative to the arts, sciences, and social struggles" (8). We are not dealing with linearity here – there is not one line that proceeds from cause to effect.

There was not one but many impulses that led to the Umbrella Movement – there was the straightforward political protest against functional constituencies, a framework whereby the voting for the Chief Executive was in the hands of 1200 representatives, there was that protest against income disparity (C.Y. Leung himself said that half of Hong Kong people earned less than US $1,800 a month), and there was the protest against the city's high property prices, insufficient provisions for public housing and the disproportionate power of property tycoons.

There was popular culture. There was art. There was also the protest against the anti-protest, against the way the students were treated. You could say that the affective tipping point for many who took to the streets was the use of pepper spray and teargas against unarmed students.

There was also a sense of festivity to the event. I am using the word "event" here in the Derridean sense. An event, Jacques Derrida reminds us, "implies surprise, exposure, the unanticipatable" (441). An event is something which we could not have prepared for, and which leaves its irreversible marks even after it is over. An event, in other words, can never be completely over and finalized.

I remember walking around Admiralty with my wife and my ten-year-old son, and it was quite a scene. Carpenters were at work making tables and chairs for study areas for the student protesters. Corporate executives were sitting on concrete road dividers and having their lunch. There were tourists taking photographs and selfies, people singing and teachers offering free English lessons. Someone even offered to massage our feet for free. He was walking around and carrying a sign that said "free foot massage".

There were well-wishers who bought provisions from the nearest supermarket so as to bring them to the various supply tents. In the words of Deleuze and Guattari, the "rhizome has no beginning or end; it is always in the middle, between things, interbeing, *intermezzo*" (27). Within the space of the Umbrella Movement, we found that intermezzo, that unlikely connection between foot massages, free English lessons and political protests.

The intermezzo is a musical term for in-between music, music between proper compositions. Occupy Central, then, was that intermezzo, in between the proper everyday life of work and study. There were people at work – putting their skills to use. You could find artists, carpenters and teachers who had set up shop in this space. There were sheltered study areas that could take up to about 400 people.

It was business as usual on the one hand, and not quite business as usual on the other. It was a space of work and study and the routines of everyday life, but it was also a suspension of everyday life. The streets were turned into art galleries.

The Umbrella Movement was an eruption of social and political desire, such that the walls of government offices were literally written over with the will of the public.

All the photographs we have seen thus far are of the Admiralty site. They were clever, allusive, and very learned. When we turn to those of the Mong Kok site, we see a slightly different scene.

There was humor there too, of course, that again was very allusive. These were the minions from the film *Despicable Me*. And these working class minions were literally manning the barricades. Blocking the streets – this was work that was anti-work, the bio-energy disrupting the flow of the capitalist regime.

There was to some extent a working class sensibility in Mong Kok. Films like *One Night in Mongkok* directed by Derek Yee, for example, had used the district as the setting for triad activities. There is also the phrase "MK tsai", referring to the Mongkok youth subculture, whose members often managed to look trendy and shabby at the same time.

The protest site at Mong Kok, like the one at Admiralty, was very canny in its display of identity. If Admiralty may roughly be said to have been the domain of the students, then at Mong Kok we saw the working class doing the work of protest – the site was often punctuated with displays of hard hats and physical labor. Displays of exhaustion were much more prominent there.

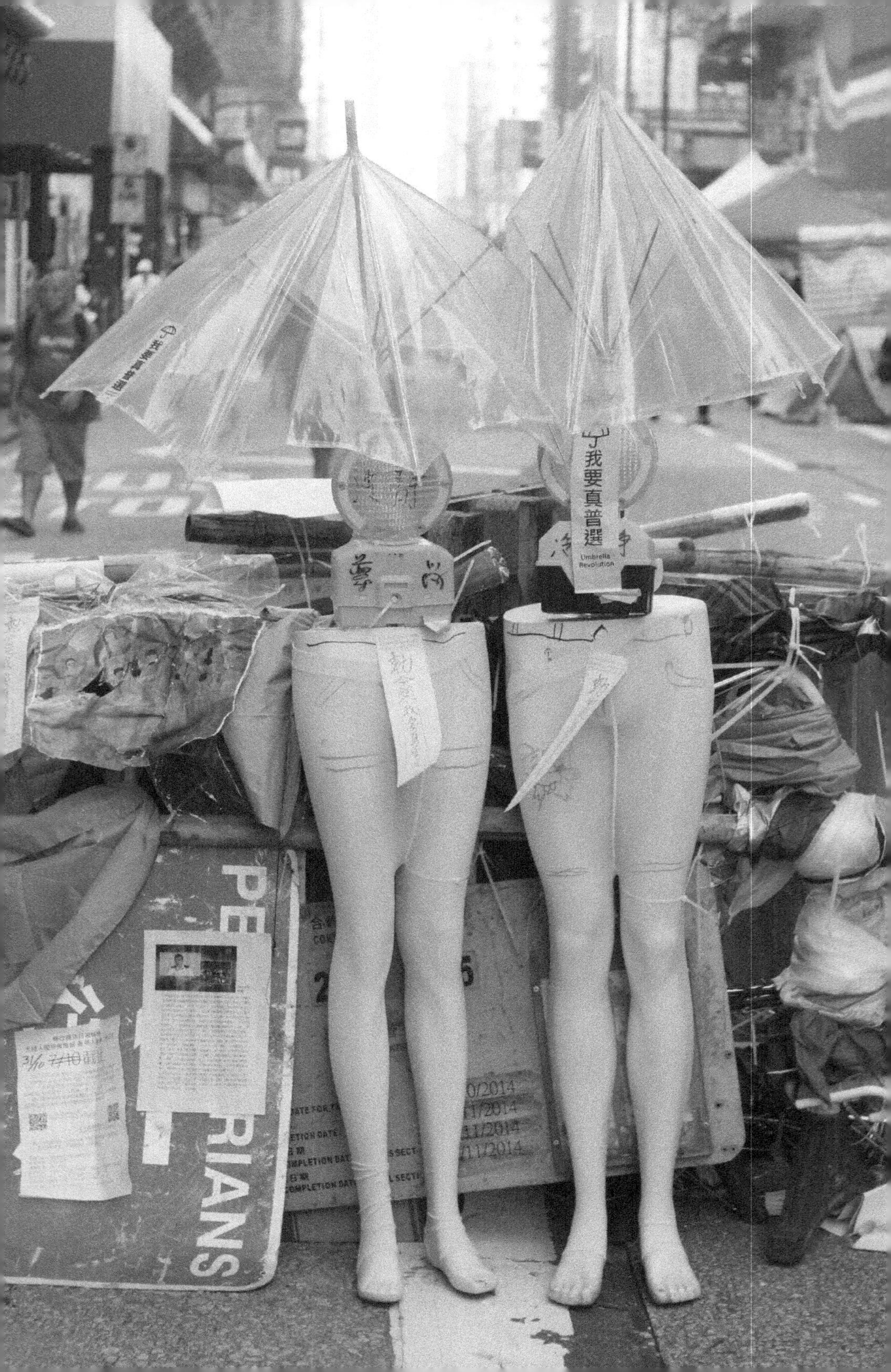
我要真普選
Umbrella Revolution
PE
RIANS

Who was responsible for exhibits like the one on the left? You could probably have identified the creators if you had tried hard enough, if you had gone around asking. Unlike the exhibits in Admiralty (such as the Umbrella Man, the wooden sculpture at the beginning of this chapter) which were presented as site-specific public art, there was a sense in Mong Kok of making do, working with materials that were repurposed.

There was the use of found objects, mass-produced objects that resulted in very witty displays. I know I cannot fully justify what I am going to say here, but at Admiralty, what we encountered was art, while at Mong Kok, we encountered displays that were not necessarily art. At least, they were not self-consciously posited as works of art, though we could read them as such. Perhaps this had to do with how the exhibits drew attention to their make-shift nature. On some days, the umbrellas were closed, and on other days, the half-mannequins were missing their stockings. Where did they go? Did they go back to the store, repurposed from their repurposing?

The image on the left was especially chilling – would this be the end result of the Umbrella Movement, I kept asking myself then. The streets of Mong Kok were somewhat rougher – on many occasions, there were anti-Occupy protesters yelling at the protesters.

On one occasion, I witnessed a woman in her forties yelling in Cantonese with a distinct mainland Chinese accent. You could spin a conspiracy theory out of this – what was a single woman trying to accomplish by stepping off the sidewalk, walking right into a group of seated male Occupy protesters and yelling at them? Was she trying to create a scene to justify police intervention? This pattern repeated itself time and again: a few of those men would rise to the bait and stand up, but their compatriots would simply say "Peace, peace, calm, calm" [和平, 和平, 冷靜, 冷靜] in Cantonese, and the scene would end with the men simply sitting back down on the ground.

As I was walking the streets of Mong Kok, I could not help but wonder at some of the displays – perhaps the Umbrella Movement was too canny for its own good. Some of the displays had the effect of reducing the protest movement into a spectacle.

Tourists would come, step off the sidewalk to take a few selfies and then go home, satisfied at having witnessed the movement.

I was, of course, complicit in this – there was probably no difference between what I was doing with my camera and what the tourists were doing.

I am reminded of Susan Sontag's point concerning photography. For her, "[p]hotography is essentially an act of non-intervention" (11). It turns everyone into a tourist. Perhaps the Umbrella Movement was too pre-occupied with images. Just as symbols may stand in for something, they may do their job too well and replace that something.

I am also reminded of Guy Debord, the author of *Society of the Spectacle*, who argues that social life is reduced to images and that our relationships are mediated via these images. Even as these displays testified to the will of the people, they stopped short at political mobilization. Debord has made the point that spectacle "is the opposite of dialogue" (6). And time and again, from the students' failed attempts at going to Beijing to engage with Chinese authorities, to how many were complaining that the Umbrella Movement had become an inconvenience to commuters and businesses, we saw how dialogue had been blocked.

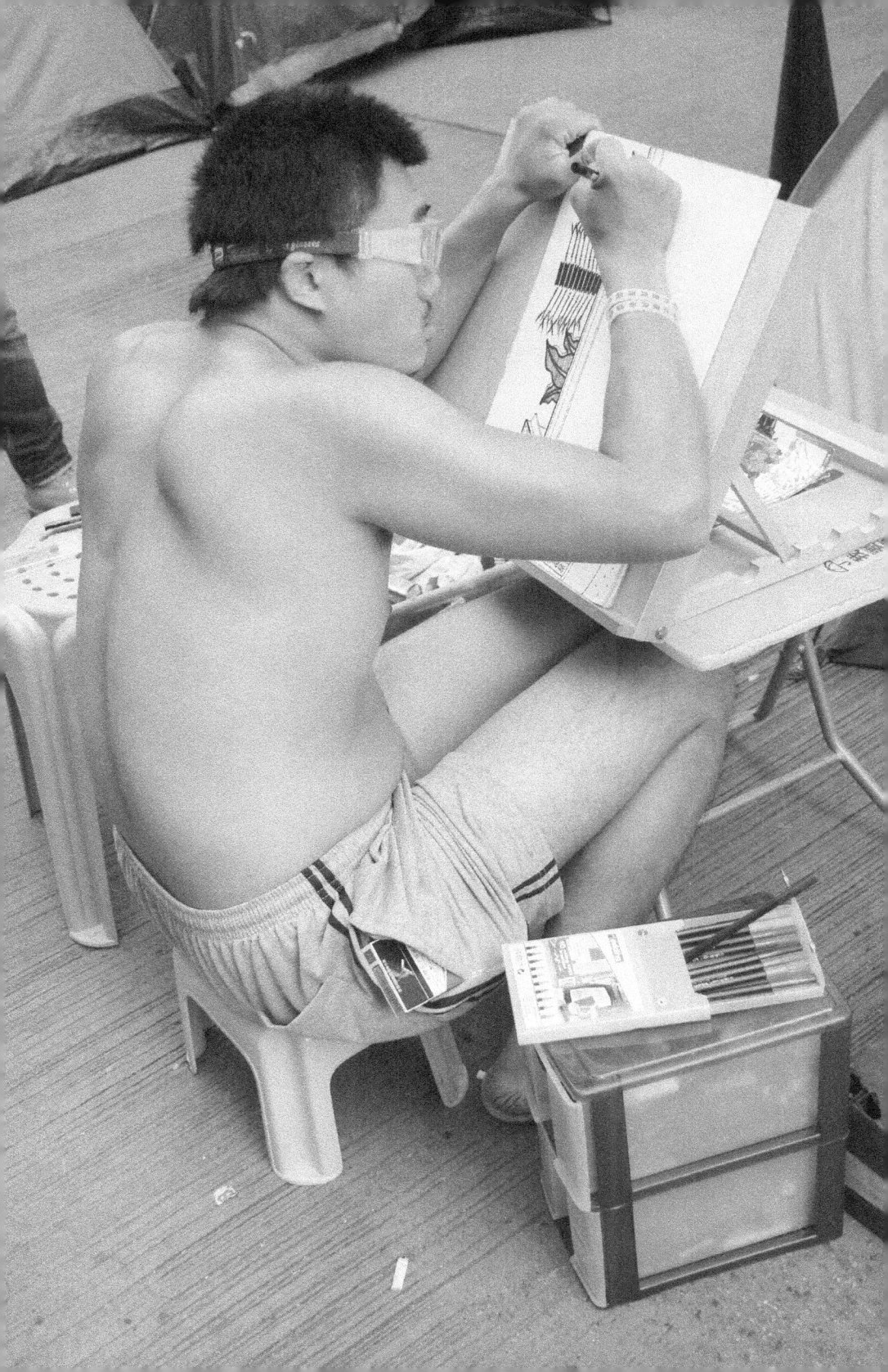

Perhaps people were too busy producing and consuming such images, to the point of forgetting the real work of revolution.

What, after all, is a revolution? Will the movement find a second wind, allowing the Umbrella Revolution to take its place in history next to the American Revolution, the French Revolution and the Velvet Revolution?

I am being very careless and glib with my remarks here, I know, but how could you have a revolution when even the police were looking so very photogenic?

Those were some of the scenes at Mong Kok. Here are some from Causeway Bay.

The Umbrella Movement was contained within the space of consumerism. It was of consumerism. Especially on the streets of Mong Kok and also at Causeway Bay, one could easily step off the occupied streets and be confronted with shops and boutiques.

Was the Umbrella Movement an event severed from everyday life, was it really discontinuous or was it simply a continuation of everyday life, imbricated in the capitalist circuits of media production and consumption? The juxtaposition of the advertising billboards with the banner was especially intriguing. As we know, the Umbrella Movement, as a physical mobilization, has come to an end. Only time will tell how Hong Kong has been transformed, or perhaps not transformed by it.

What was Hong Kong occupied by in those 79 days?

It was occupied by images.

Perhaps it was occupied by simulacrum of a revolution, rather than the revolution itself.

You could see that I am caught in a net of ambivalence.

On the one hand, the Umbrella Movement was the articulation of a public will, a mobilization for the cause of genuine universal suffrage. It was decentralized, consisting of various networks of people. In this way, it was a rhizomatic event that can never be fully eradicated. Again, let me quote Deleuze and Guattari:

> A rhizome may be broken, shattered at a given spot, but it will start
> up again on one of its old lines, or on new lines. You can never get
> rid of ants because they form an animal rhizome that can rebound
> time and again after most of it has been destroyed (10).

The Umbrella Movement could also be seen as an eruption that characterized the relationship between nations as imagined communities and the legal–political machinery of the state. It was a moment when governmental apparatuses found themselves interrogated by the will of the people. If you think of it this way, then there is hope for change. As it says on the Lennon Wall, "even if you're disappointed, you can't lose hope".

On the other hand, there was the hyperreality of the movement, mediated via signs and symbols and imagery; perhaps you could even say that the movement was largely made out of signs and symbols and imagery and nothing else. The media of the movement became more prominent than the movement itself. Jean

Baudrillard had said that the Gulf War did not take place. It was not really a war because it was conducted via remote video imagery and media presentations. Could we say the same of the Umbrella Movement? Was it real? Did it really take place?

Perhaps the Umbrella Movement was the appearance of politics, and at the same time, the disappearance of politics.

The ambivalence I feel towards the Umbrella Movement is a public ambivalence.

There are some who say that nothing has changed.

There are others who say that everything has changed.

STREET MEDITATIONS

There is what Michel de Certeau calls the "absent figure", a figure created by techniques and rationalities that govern the everyday life of the city (vi). For de Certeau, the absent figure is the product of quantification, of "computations and rationalities" that govern urban life (vi). This notion of the absent figure points to a social as well as an existential condition, a condition whereby something (or someone) has meaning only if it is expressed in terms of numbers. To give this a Marxist slant, the absent figure is alienated from his life through quantification, be it the size of a bank account, the worth of a residential property or a salary.

De Certeau's notion of the absent figure is especially applicable to Hong Kong, a city that continues to be self-evident as a particular geopolitical site of economic opportunities for global corporations, and it may be argued that capitalism, both local and global, is too often posited as a solution, however inadequate, to the anxieties attending to its political future. One may argue that Hong Kong people are absent figures caught between the grids of economic rationalities and its particular historical situation. Ackbar Abbas has made the point that in Hong Kong the "sense of the temporary" is very strong (4). Since the 1984 Sino-British Joint Declaration, everyday life is held in deferral to 1997, and since 1997, the everyday present is once again suspended and held in deference to the year 2046. Tiananmen in 1989 exacerbated the anxieties of many concerning Hong Kong's postcolonial future. Decisive historical junctures led to indecisive everyday moments, moments that many sought to escape through emigration in the years leading up to 1997. Hence, in her poem "Island", Ho writes of Hong Kong first as a "floating island" and later as a "city with a country / An international city becoming national" (*Incense Tree* 109). The ambivalence and indecisive moments in the poem have to do with how it oscillates between anxiety and security concerning the status of Hong Kong as part of China. The poem is still relevant today: the Umbrella Movement was in part the response of an international city becoming national.

Hong Kong is, to again use Benedict Anderson's formulation, an "imagined community" of absent figures (6). Yet there is a possibility of retrieving everyday life from the social, physical and cultural spaces of Hong Kong. De Certeau has made the point that "[e]veryday life invents itself by *poaching* in countless ways on the property of others" [italics in original] (xii). Everyday life is transgressive, in that meaning has to be salvaged, on the sly, from in-between (and often indecisive) moments of the grand narratives of history and capitalism. Such is the given condition of aesthetic production in Hong Kong. If art is about the salvaging of meaning, then it is in league with everyday life, to the extent that artistic works become transgressive and predatory mediums.

In the series of meditations that follows, poems and photographs are regarded as forms usurping the material spaces of Hong Kong. In this way, one is led to consider the possibilities of cultural production as a kind of furtive production wherein everyday life in Hong Kong is made to speak:

No one sees the mental life of cities.

No one denies it is there.

It is darkness on the streets.

It is impulsive as pigeons.

I am a camera
hunting for metaphors. (Tay *Mental Life* 2)

THE HUMDRUM

There are many possibilities to the above scene. What led to that glance? That second look, from the woman to the man. A second thought: what is he doing? What is he looking for? Who is he? An indecisive moment where many things are possible. He seems to be working. But what is the nature of his work? The couple seems to be on a stroll. But why are they at leisure in this rather unprepossessing landscape? The point is not to answer these questions. There is no doubt that the answers might disappoint and return us to the humdrum.

Roland Barthes has made the point that there is "something tautological" about a "specific photograph" in that it "is never distinguished from its referent" (*Camera Lucida* 5). But a street photographer does not produce a specific photograph. A family portrait, a travel photograph of children set against a recognizable tourist landscape, a photograph of a model holding a luxury handbag in a magazine, a photograph accompanying a newspaper report – these are specific photographs, tautological. A street photograph strains against tautology because it is deprived of its denotative quality. There is, in the end, no lexical "street". The absent figures in the above photograph are made to enter a connotative space. What is being spoken here is another reality, a reality that is accumulating in the form of non-answers. It is a suspended moment rendered unreal, an accretion of silence. We are viewing a spreading void. But the figures are now present. They have been made significant.

But for the street photographer, the void dissipates too quickly and he is returned to the humdrum, perhaps reminded of an errand, a bill to be paid, or of the work that awaits him at his office.

THE *FLÂNEUR*

For there are many techniques and demands of living operating their effects on the street photographer: ranging from "a father", "a consumer of camera products", "a hobbyist with artistic pretensions", "a husband entrusted with an errand". The street photographer is necessarily furtive: he is not a properly socialized figure. He steals moments from everyday routines – fifteen minutes here, thirty minutes there, while waiting for his spouse to be done with her shopping, on his way home, on his way to the office. Street photography is not a proper profession; at best, it is something attached to a professional photography career. It is not surprising to find a professional photographer who looks upon his or her street photography as "personal work", the implication of which is that it is otherwise not proper for him or her to do such work.

The street photographer, then, is akin to a poet in that there is likewise no proper social role ascribed to him or her. Who in Hong Kong is a poet? I know of English language poets who are teachers, who work in publishing, who work for non-profit companies, and in one case, who is a vintage car mechanic. How then does one accumulate and produce aesthetic experience as a poet, beyond what

Walter Benjamin calls "the standardized, denatured life of the civilized masses" (*Charles Baudelaire: A Lyric Poet* 110)? What I find interesting is that to Benjamin's *flâneur*, "the shiny, enamelled signs of businesses are at least as good a wall ornament as an oil painting is to a bourgeois in his salon" (*Charles Baudelaire: A Lyric Poet* 37).

What, then, may we learn from Benjamin's *flâneur*?:

Sometimes I get tired of walking around.

Sometimes I think there is no use
stalking after nouns in this city,
where buildings are cut like glass.

Our houses take on conveniences
of pigeonholes, square as a blueprint.
There are no words on the pavement,
not even whispers of leaves –
our city planners took care of them.

Sometimes I get tired of walking around,
of shopping, of posters,
of cafes and blinking lights,
of streets leading me to a blind corner.

At dawn, when the people arise
and go about their business,
lamp-posts tremble and die,
repeating themselves like question marks. (Tay *Remnants* 39)

In the above, even as the persona is lamenting the standardized and reified nature of urban life, the poem relies on these very same standardized and reified images to make its point. The street photograph shares the same condition, in that the commonplace is made to be more than itself.

THE APATHETIC

Even as he draws from these standardized and reified images, what frightens the street photographer is the apathy of the absent figures to their material environment. The sense impressions of the absent figure are hardened against the material surface of his or her environment. Everything is regarded as commonplace, looked over quickly and overlooked.

How may we read the following photograph except as a work of anxiety?

This photograph is made possible because of the framing which highlights the rectilinear grids out of an otherwise larger and unappealing urban landscape. Even as the street photographer salvages the rectilinear logic and arrangement of the colours from the scene with his frame, he could see that no one sees. Even as he looks at the photograph he remembers the questioning looks from those outside the frame. A street photograph for the one who took it is a reminder of the everyday experience of aesthetic production. There was a trash collector who looked at him suspiciously. Framing is an anxious, self-conscious and lonely act.

Yet the *flâneur* takes pleasure in moments exemplified above. He transforms the bodily movement of the absent figure into an aesthetic effect; the human figure is dark against the solidity of the background. Perhaps taking a photograph such as the one above is also a defiant act. The apathetic figure in the above photograph is blurred, rendered transient and temporary in relation to the background. One cannot help but note the paradox: even though she completes the photograph, the anonymous absent figure is not supposed to be in the picture.

Another possibility: the figure on the photograph is the disavowed double of the one taking the photograph. The street photographer fears he is taking a portrait of himself. Why does one write? Why does one feel the need to take photographs? What is the cause of the aesthetic impulse? Hence, the following lines from Kate Rogers:

> I am full of holes:
> Each orifice gapes its need: fill me.
> I am falling into the holes,
> trying to catch myself on the edge
> of disappearance. (*City of Stairs* 72)

Except for moments when they are writing or taking photographs, the poet and the photographer are themselves blurred and vague absent figures on the verge of fading.

TACTICS

Perhaps writing poetry and shooting street photographs are tactics forestalling those moments when one has to fade into the work of institutions, demand and supply of markets, maintaining of disciplines, systems of power, and fields of technique. If poetry and street photography (and art in general) have a social role, it seems to be a role against forces larger than themselves. Yet is the aesthetic moment to be regarded simply as the small against the large, the marginal against the dominant, the frail against the powerful?

De Certeau has made much of the opposition between tactic and strategies. For him, "a *tactic* is a calculated action determined by the absence of a proper locus", one deployed by someone who has no proper place of practice, no proper institutional recognition, and who is in a weaker position [italics in original] (de

Certeau 36 – 37). A tactician does not accumulate: "What it wins it cannot keep" (de Certeau 37). In contrast, a strategy belongs to establishments, authorities, and "systems and totalizing discourses" (de Certeau 38). It is "organized by the postulation of power" (de Certeau 38). But surely one can be both a strategist and tactician at the same time:

Quietly, quietly,
it is the other one
who does not believe in work.

When I wish my colleagues good morning,
he sleeps soundlessly in my bed.

When I talk to clients,
he mumbles *why bother* in his dreams.

Quietly, quietly,
it is the other one,
the one who shares my name,
who does not belong.

His room, dusty and littered with laundry,
is not my room.

My room is tidy and objective.
I have tried many times to chase him out.

When I come home with my packet of dinner,
he wakes up, rubs his eyes
and snatches it from me.

He puts on my clothes, steals my money, and tells me
I have measured out my life with coffee spoons.

When I go to bed hungry
he leaves the house with my keys
and prowls the night for poetry.

His streets are not my streets.
I am afraid to talk to him.

He pastes messages on my computer,
messages I could not understand.

Especially the one telling me to go with him
when the evening is spread out against the sky
like a patient etherised upon a table.

Mornings, just as I am waking up,
he opens the door and throws the keys at me.

Quietly, quietly,
when he tosses and turns in my bed,
I leave the house and go about my business.
(Tay *A Lover's Soliloquy* 70-71)

The above poem exemplifies how the poet inevitably partakes in the pedestrian. One may say the same of the street photographer as well. The poet and street photographer know too well how they themselves are adept collaborators within a larger system. By virtue of their literacy skills and ownership of cameras with technical specifications adequate to their tasks, more often than not, they belong to a somewhat privileged class. The poet is educated, is an educator, is literate and cultivated, is recognizable within publishing, academic, cultural and institutional circuits of poetry reading. The street photographer operates and identifies himself within a genre of photo-books spanning from Henri Cartier-Bresson to contemporary luminaries such as Stephen Shore, Tod Papageorge and Martin Parr. Tactics and strategies are not mutually opposed. Rather, individual and isolated tactics are made possible through the study of accumulated strategies.

INTERIORITY

Tactics and accumulated strategies – do they give rise to aesthetic occasions? The pleasure of aesthetic experience, whether it is the act of writing or reading, whether it is the act of taking or viewing street photographs, is interior, unrecognizable to another, and there is no description or theoretical exposition that does justice to it.

Shigeo Gocho:

> Sometimes, in the background behind the varied surface of the
> everyday, the inexplicable shadow of human existence creeps in
> like a fog. This shadow gets trapped at the barrier between what
> is expressible through words and what is not, accumulating like an
> unanswered riddle in the hollow of spreading emptiness, as if it is
> becoming some sort of creature that continues to multiply within
> the opaque whirlpool that is the everyday. (52–53)

Is such an interiority possible within the whirlpool of everyday that is Hong
Kong? Hong Kong is constructed out of massive structures in accordance to
a rational urban planning that extracts maximum spatial efficiency. Given its
high population density, Hong Kong people are highly disciplined, their bodies
governed by regulatory laws of walking that pervade public horizontal spaces.

De Certeau writes optimistically of a kind of walking which "creates a
mobile organicity in the environment"; for him, "[w]alking affirms, suspects,
tries out, transgresses, respects, etc., the trajectories it 'speaks'" (99). But is such a
pleasurable and leisurely mobile organicity possible in Hong Kong? In the above

scene, so ubiquitous to Hong Kong's urban environment, walking cannot be anything else apart from being functional. Horizontal paths have been laid out for both pedestrians and drivers. There is no such thing as an unplanned horizon in the city. Likewise, there is a vertical spatial discipline at work which organizes residential and commercial spaces into neat compartments. People are caught within a grid even as they are walking, eating, sleeping, working, waiting, talking, buying and selling.

The convergence between selves and the city is complete and total; just as walking is predetermined by city planners, the pathways of the mind are predetermined by capitalistic drives. As previously mentioned, in "The Metropolis and Mental Life", Georg Simmel argues that in the city, "those irrational, instinctive, sovereign traits and impulses which aim at determining the mode of life from within" are eradicated or at the very least, suppressed (*Sociology* 413). The form of life that is possible in Hong Kong is mostly received from the exterior. This regimental exteriority organized by rationality and efficiency discipline the bodies and minds of the absent figures, to the extent that interiority is dissolved or at least, held hostage to the pedestrian concerns of making a living. Even as one feels the hollow of a spreading emptiness, there is no unanswered riddle.

THE BODY AT LABOR

Capitalism has become an alibi for the unexamined life. What is at stake is technique and a confidence that only a body at labor is able to possess. The paint flakes on the back of the man in the following photograph is a sign of the dominion of labor over the physical body.

In the section on docile bodies in *Discipline and Punish*, Michel Foucault writes of "the protected space of disciplinary monotony" (141). This space is distinguished from others so as to make concrete the work of discipline. He writes of "disciplinary space" that is "cellular" (Foucault *Discipline* 143). The lorry has become that mobile cellular space with the human body as adjunct. As Foucault puts it, "[d]iscipline is…a whole set of instruments, techniques, procedures, levels of application, targets" (*Discipline* 215). Hence, it makes no sense to talk of self-discipline apart from a self that internalizes the discipline enabled by agents, agendas and processes in collusion with the self.

It is tempting to aestheticize the above moment through the photograph. How may the above moment be rendered in the photograph as a work of critique? The photograph is silent, and perhaps this marks the limit of the photographer who wants to do more. On the other hand, there is, I admit, a sort of authorial arrogance that contrasts the work of the photographer, academic and poet with manual work. Is it possible to inhabit the space of what has been captured, for the photographed to look back at the photographer, for those written about to retort the writer? Is the author writing only to himself, the photographer taking pictures only of himself?

THE FUGITIVE COMMUNITY

There is of course the possibility of a community within Hong Kong. One sees pockets of micro-communities brought together by mutual interests. One might argue for a fugitive space that is carved out of an otherwise public and commercial space. The community is like the table - provisional, makeshift, tentative. This is friendship outside a food stall. This is a space of concentration and familiarity.

At times, it seems like everything in Hong Kong is governed by the hegemony of property ownership. A business lives and dies by its lease with its landlord. Middle-class families are made peripatetic in search of more affordable leasing contracts for their flats, while the relatively less privileged are anchored down by routinized menial work and highly-subsidized public housing.

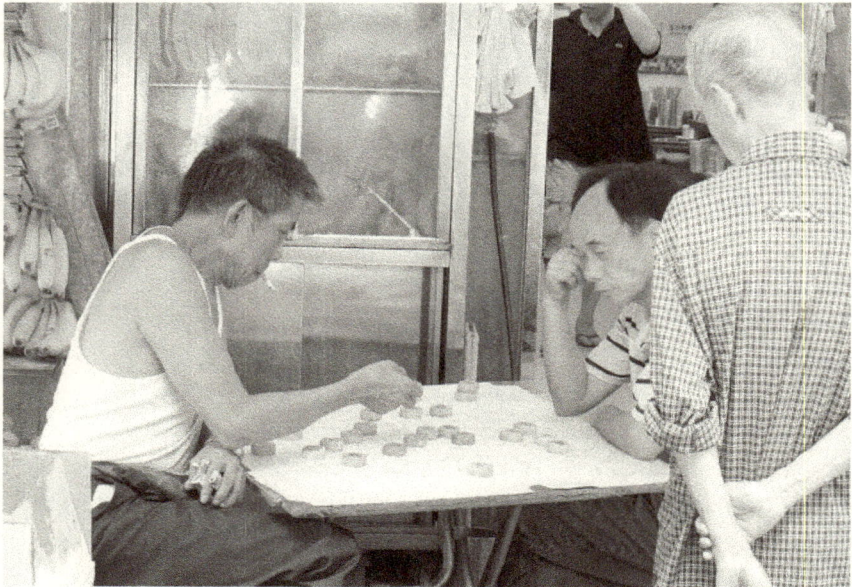

Perhaps the poet-photographer-academic is being stubbornly naïve, his discussion revolving around artistic production and social structures of Hong Kong. But in the end, one cannot help but pursue an art that is linked to the local community and informed by engagements with critical concepts. De Certeau's notion of everyday life is that for it to be meaningful, it has to be snatched from powerful grips of capitalism, grand ideological apparatuses and institutions that do not work in the interests of what it means to be human. One of the aims here is to explore the kinds of knowledge that the reading and writing of poetry as well as the taking and viewing of street photographs can offer. In the end, there are no claims to grand visions. What emerges is a constellation of nodes: the humdrum, the *flâneur*, the apathetic, tactics, interiority, the laboring body and the possibility of a fugitive community; a resistance against closure, restless acts of seeing, reading, understanding, in the hope that an argument might be made that the lives of absent figures bear examination.

AFTERWORD: GETTING A WAY

This book is an art-making project that blends scholarship, personal anecdotes, poetry and street photography into a practice. You could say that I am improvising, working with various genres, searching for a language that is both literary and critical. We need ways to talk about what it is that drives us as writers and artists.

I believe in the work of scholarship, because it is a discipline that compels us to think critically with ideas. I believe in getting personal, because artistic practice takes place via the self's engagement with the environment. I believe in poetry, because everyday language as a medium is too generic. To speak about the self is to speak a personal language, and that is the domain of poetry. I believe in street photography, because it teaches us to look outwards, for moments of visual poetry in the external environment.

Both Hong Kong and Singapore are cities subject to capitalist desires, institutional discourses and state power. We are workers, consumers and citizens. These identities do not always work in our interests; they do not always help us think about what it means to lead a meaningful life. Given this, as Foucault reminds us, "there is only one practical consequence: we have to create ourselves as a work of art" (1983/1997: 262). This book has been a meaning-making project in response to a life lived in these two cities. If anything, it celebrates a kind of restlessness out of which one can artfully speak.

WORKS CITED

Abbas, Ackbar. *Hong Kong: Culture and the Politics of Disappearance*. Hong Kong: Hong Kong UP, 1997.

Academy of Visual Arts, Hong Kong Baptist University. "Umbrella Patchwork – An Impressive Installation Artwork by AVA Students". [http://ava.hkbu.edu.hk/2014/10/%E2%80%9Cumbrella-patchwork%E2%80%9D-in-admiralty/]. Accessed 31st Dec 2014.

Alfian Sa'at. *One Fierce Hour*. Singapore: Landmark Books, 1998.

Anderson, Benedict. *Imagined Communities: Reflections on the Origin and Spread of Nationalism*. Revised ed. London: Verso, 2006. [1983]

Anderson, Leon. "Analytic Autoethnography". *Journal of Contemporary Ethnography*. 35.4 (2006): 373-395.

Ang, Ien . *On Not Speaking Chinese: Living between Asia and the West*. London: Routledge, 2001.

Ashcroft, Bill, et al. *The Empire Writes Back*. London: Routledge, 2002.

Asian Literary Review. Hong Kong: Print Work.

Attridge, Derek. "Innovation, Literature, Ethics: Relating to the Other". *PMLA* 114.1 (1999): 20-31.

Atkinson, Paul. "Rescuing Autoethnography". *Journal of Contemporary Ethnography*. 35.4 (2006): 400-404.

Barthes, Roland. *Camera Lucida: Reflections of Photography*. Trans. Richard Howard. London: Vintage, 2000. [New York: Hill and Wang, 1981].

---. *Image-Music-Text*. Trans. Stephen Heath. London: Fontana, 1977.

---. *Mythologies*. Trans. Annette Lavers. New York: Hill and Wang, 1972. [1957].

Baudrillard, Jean. *The Ecstasy of Communication*. Trans. Bernard Schütze and Caroline Schütze. Los Angeles, CA: Semiotext(e), 2012. [1987].

---. *The Gulf War Did Not Take Place*. Trans. Paul Patton. Bloomington: Indiana UP, 1995.
Beckett, Samuel. *Molloy; Mallone Dies; The Unnamable*. New York: Alfred A. Knopf, 1997.

Benjamin, Walter. *Charles Baudelaire: A Lyric Poet in the Era of High Capitalism*. Trans. Harry Zohn. London; New York: Verso, 1997.

---. *Illuminations*. Trans. Harry Zohn. New York: Shocken, 1968. [1955]

---. *The Writer of Modern Life: Essays on Charles Baudelaire*. Ed. Michael W. Jennings. Trans. Howard Eiland, Edmund Jephcott, Rodney Livingstone and Harry Zohn. Cambridge, Massachusetts: The Belknap Press of Harvard UP, 2006.

Berger, John and Jean Mohr. *Another Way of Telling.* New York: Vintage, 1995. [1982]

Blunt, Alison. "Geography and the Humanities Tradition". *Key Concepts in Geography.* 2nd ed. Eds. Nicholas J. Clifford, Sarah L. Holloway, Stephen P. Rice and Gill Valentine. London: SAGE, 2009. 67-82.

Boey, Kim Cheng. *Between Stations.* New South Wales, Australia: Giramondo, 2009.

Bolton, Kingsley. "The Sociolinguistics of Hong Kong and the Space for Hong Kong English". *World Englishes* 19.3 (2000): 265-285.

Bradsher, Keith and Chris Buckley. "Hong Kong Leader Affirms Unbending Stance" *New York Times.* 20th Oct 2014. [http://www.nytimes.com/2014/10/21/world/asia/leung-chun-ying-hong-kong-china-protests.html?_r=0] Accessed 31 Dec 2014.

Bynner, Witter. "To One Unnamed". James Kraft, ed. *The Works of Witter Bynner.* New York: Farrar Straus Giroux, 1978. 127.

Carney, John. "Perry Dino Captures Hong Kong's Protests in Oil on Canvas". *South China Morning Post.* 23rd Sept 2012. [http://www.scmp.com/lifestyle/arts-culture/article/1043353/perry-dino-captures-hong-kong-protests-oil-canvas] Accessed 31 Dec 2014.

Cartier-Bresson, Henri. *The Decisive Moment.* New York: Simon and Schuster, 1952.

de Certeau, Michel. *The Practice of Everyday Life.* Trans. Steven Rendall. Berkeley, California: U of California P, 1984

Cha: An Asian Literary Journal. [http://www.asiancha.com/] Accessed 01.06.10.

Chin, Grace. V. S. "The Anxieties of Authorship in Malaysian and Singaporean Writings in English: Locating the English Language Writer and the Question of Freedom in the Postcolonial Era". *Postcolonial Text* 2.4: (2006): 1-24.

Chua, Beng Huat. "Multiculturalism in Singapore: An Instrument of Social Control". *Race & Class* 44.3 (2003): 58-77.

---. "Public Housing Residents as Clients of the State". *Housing Studies.* 15.1 (2000): 45-60.

Chua, Chee Lay, ed. *Keeping My Mandarin Alive: Lee Kuan Yew's Language Learning Experience.* Singapore: World Scientific, 2005.

Cixious, Hélène and Mireille Calle-Gruber. Trans. Eric Prenowitz. *Hélène Cixious, Rootprints: Memory and Life Writing.* London, New York: Routledge, 1997. [1994].

Clarke, David. *Chinese Art and its Encounter with the World.* Hong Kong: Hong Kong UP, 2011.

Davison, Chris and Winnie Y. W. Auyeung Lai. "Competing Identities, Common Issues: Teaching (in) Putonghua". *Language Policy* 6 (2009): 119-134.

Debord, Guy. Trans. Ken Knabb. *Society of the Spectacle*. Berkeley CA: Bureau of Public Secrets, 2014. [1967]

Deleuze, Gilles and Félix Guattari. Trans. Brian Massumi. *A Thousand Plateaus: Capitalism and Schizophrenia*. London: Continuum, 1987. [1980]

Derrida, Jacques. Trans. Gila Walker. "A Certain Impossible Possibility of Saying the Event". *Critical Inquiry*, Vol. 33, No. 2 (Winter 2007), pp. 441-461.

Despicable Me. Dir. Pierre Coffin and Chris Renaud. Perf. Steve Carell, Jason Segall and Russell Brand. Universal Pictures, 2010. Film.

Dixon, L. Quentin. "Bilingual Education Policy in Singapore: An Analysis of its Sociohistorical Roots and Current Academic Outcomes". *International Journal of Bilingual Education and Bilingualism* 8.1 (2005): 25-47.

Elden, Stuart. *Understanding Henri Lefebvre: Theory and the Possible*. London: Continuum, 2004.

Elkins, James. *The Object Stares Back*. London: Harcourt, 1996.

---, ed. *What Do Artists Know?* Pennsylvania, USA: The Pennsylvania State University Press, 2012.

Ellis, Carolyn S. and Arthur Bochner. "Analyzing Analytic Autoethnography: An Autopsy". *Journal of Contemporary Ethnography*. 35.4 (2006): 429-449.

Fan, Kit. *Paper Scissors Stone*. Hong Kong: Hong Kong UP, 2011.

Fenza, David. 2011. "The Centre Has Not Held: Creative Writing & Pluralism". *New Writing: The International Journal for the Practice and Theory of Creative Writing* 8, no. 3: 206-214.

Fernando, Lloyd. *Cultures in Conflict: Essays on Literature and the English Language in South East Asia*. Singapore: Graham Brash, 1986.

Firth, Alan. "The Lingua Franca Factor". *Intercultural Pragmatics* 6.2 (2009): 147-170.

Fish, Stanley. "Boutique Multiculturalism, or Why Liberals are Incapable of Thinking about Hate Speech". *Critical Inquiry* 23.2 (1997): 378-395.

Foucault, Michel. *Discipline and Punish: The Birth of the Prison*. Trans. Alan Sheridan. London: Penguin, 1977. [1975]

---. "Madness, the Absence of Work". Trans. Peter Stastny and Deniz engel. *Critical Inquiry*. 21. 2 (1995): 290-298.

---. "On the Genealogy of Ethics: An Overview of Work in Progress." Paul Rabinow, ed. Trans. Robert Hurley. *The Essential Works of Foucault, 1954–1984, Vol I: Ethics, Subjectivity and Truth.* New York: The Free Press, 1997. 253-280. [1983]

Freire, Paulo. *Pedagogy of the Oppressed.* New York; London: Continuum, 2005. [1970]

Garrard, Greg. *Ecocriticism.* London: Routledge, 2004.

Geertz, Clifford. *The Interpretation of Cultures.* New York: Basic Books, 1973.

Gill, Sauran Kaur. "Language Policy in Malaysia: Reversing Direction". *Language Policy 4* (2005): 241-260.

Gocho, Shigeo. "Photograph as Another Reality". *Setting Sun: Writings by Japanese Photographers.* Eds Ivan Vartanian, Akihiro Hatanaka and Yutaka Kambayashi. New York: Aperture, 2006. 52-53.

Goh, Robbie B. H. "Imagining the Nation: The Role of Singapore Poetry in English in 'Emergent Nationalism'". *Journal of Commonwealth Literature.* 41.2 (2006): 21-41.

---. "The Anxiety of Influences: Dis-locating Authority, Culture and Identity in the Novels of Colin Cheong". *Journal of Commonwealth Literature* 42.3 (2007): 45-62.

Golding, William. *Lord of the flies.* United Kingdom: Faber, 1954.

Gwee, Li Sui. "The New Poetry of Singapore". Gwee (ed.) *Sharing Borders: Studies in Contemporary Singaporean-Malaysian literature II.* Singapore: National Library Board, 2009. 236-259.

Heidegger, Martin. *Poetry, Language, Thought.* Trans. Albert Hofstadter. New York: Harper and Row, 1975.

Ho, Elaine Yee Lin. "Language Policy, 'Asia's World City' and Anglophone Hong Kong Writing". *Interventions: International Journal of Postcolonial Studies* 12.3 (2010): 428-441.

Ho, Louise. "Hong Kong Writing and Writing Hong Kong". In K. Bolton, ed. Hong Kong English: Autonomy and Creativity. Hong Kong: Hong Kong UP, 2001. 173-179.

---. *Incense Tree: Collected Poems of Louise Ho.* Hong Kong: Hong Kong UP, 2009.

Ho, Tammy. (2010) "Bathing in a Ski-Suit: Writing in a Second Language." *Cha: An Asian Literary Journal.* On WWW at http://www.asiancha.com/index.php?option=com_content&task=blogcategory&id=107&Itemid=241. Accessed 15.06.10.

Horkheimer, Max and Theodor W. Adorno. Trans John Cumming. *Dialectic of Enlightenment.* New York: Continuum, 1999. [1944].

Hugo, Victor. *Les Misérables.* New York: Signet, 2013. [1862]

Keats, John. *The Letters of John Keats, 1814-1821*. Volume 1. Ed. Hyder Edward Rollins. Cambridge, MA: Harvard UP, 1958.

Kerr, Douglas. "Louise Ho and the Local Turn: The Place of English Poetry in Hong Kong". Ed. Kam Louie. *Hong Kong Culture: Word and Image*. Hong Kong: Hong Kong University Press, 2010. 75-95.

Lai, Mee-ling. "Hong Kong Students' Attitudes towards Cantonese, Putonghua and English after the Change of Sovereignty". *Journal of Multilingual and Multicultural Development* 22.2 (2001): 112-133.

Lam, Agnes. "Defining Hong Kong Poetry in English". K. Bolton (ed.) *Hong Kong English: Autonomy and Creativity*. Hong Kong: Hong Kong UP, 2001. 183-197.

Latham, Alan, Derek McCormack, Kim McNamara and Donald McNeill. *Key Concepts in Urban Geography*. London: SAGE, 2009.

Lee, Francis L. F. "Collective Efficacy, Support for Democratization, and Political Participation in Hong Kong". *International Journal of Public Opinion Research* 18.3 (2005): 297-317.

Lee, Tzu Pheng. "My Country and My People". Society of Singapore Writers (ed.) *Tides of Memories and Other Singapore Poems*. Singapore: Asiapac Books, 2002. [1976]. 104-106.
Lefebvre, Henri. *The Production of Space*. Trans. Donald Nicholson-Smith. Oxford: Blackwell Publishers, 1991.

Leung, Ping-Kwan. "Writing between Chinese and English". K. Bolton (ed.) *Hong Kong English: Autonomy and Creativity*. Hong Kong: Hong Kong UP, 2001. 199-205.

Lévi-Strauss, Claude. *The Savage Mind*. London: Weidenfeld and Nicolson, 1966.

Lim, Shirley Geok-lin. *Writing S. E. / Asia in English: Against the Grain, Focus on Asian English-language Literature*. London: Skoob, 1994.

---. "English-Language Creative Writing in Hong Kong: Colonial Stereotype and Process". *Pedagogy: Critical Approaches to Teaching Literature, Language, Composition, and Culture* 1.1 (2001): 178-184.

---. "Lore, Practice, and Social Identity in Creative Writing Pedagogy: Speaking with a Yellow Voice?". *Pedagogy: Critical Approaches to Teaching Literature, Language, Composition, and Culture* 10.1 (2010): 79-93.

---. *Monsoon History: Selected Poems*. London: Skoob, 1994.

---. "The Im/possibility of Life-writing in Two Languages". De Courtivron, Isabelle, ed. *Lives in Translation: Bilingual Writers on Identity and Creativity*. New York: Palgrave Macmillan, 2003. 39-47.

Lin, Angel Mei Yi. "Analyzing the 'Language Problem' Discourse in Hong Kong: How Official, Academic, and Media Discourses Construct and Perpetuate Dominant Models of Language, Learning, and Education. *Journal of Pragmatics* 28 (1997): 427-40.

Ma, Eric Kit-wai. *Desiring Hong Kong, Consuming South China: Transborder Cultural Politics,* 1970-2010. Hong Kong: Hong Kong UP, 2012.

McLuhan, Marshall and Jerome Agel. *The Medium is the Massage.* London: Penguin, 1996. [1967]

Ministry of Information and the Arts. (2010) *The Renaissance City Report: Culture and the Arts in Renaissance Singapore.* [http://app.mica.gov.sg/Portals/0/2_FinalRen.pdf.] Accessed 17.03.10.

Ministry of Information, Communications and the Arts (MICA). *Renaissance City Plan III.* Singapore: MICA, 2008.

Nair, Chandran. *Once the Horsemen and Other Poems.* Singapore: U Education P., 1972.

Nehamas, Alexander. Nietzsche: Life as literature. Cambridge, Massachusetts: Harvard UP, 1985.
One Night in Mongkok. Dir. Derek Yee. Perf. Cecilia Cheing, Danial Wu and Alex Fong. Film Unlimited, 2004. Film.

Ong, Aihwa. *Flexible Citizenship: The Cultural Logics of Transnationality.* Durham and London: Duke UP, 1999.

Orwell, George. *Nineteen Eighty-Four.* New York: Harcourt, Brace [1949].

Pang, Alvin, ed. *Tumasik.* Singapore: National Arts Council of Singapore; Iowa City, USA: Autumn Hills Books; Iowa City, USA: International Writing Program at the U of Iowa, 2009.

Pang, Alvin and Tiziano Fratus, eds. *Double Skin: New Poetic Voices from Italy and Singapore.* Singapore: Ethos, 2009.

Pang, Alvin. and John Kinsella, eds. *Over There: Poems from Australia and Singapore.* Singapore: Ethos, 2008.

Pang, Alvin and Aaron Lee, A, eds. *No Other City: The Ethos Anthology of Urban Poetry.* Singapore: Ethos, 2000.

Pang, Alvin, et al, eds. *Love Gathers All: The Philippines-Singapore Anthology of Love.* Philippines: Anvil Publishing; Singapore: Ethos, 2002.

Pang, Laikwan. *Creativity and its Discontents: China's Creative Industries and Intellectual Property Rights Offenses.* Durham: Duke UP, 2012.

Patke, Rajeev. "Voice and Authority in English Poetry from Singapore". *Interlogue: Studies in Singapore Literature, Volume 2: Poetry.* Ed. Kirpal Singh. Singapore: Ethos, 1999. 85-103.

Pennycook, Alastair. "Teaching with the Flow: Fixity and Fluidity in Education". *Asia Pacific Journal of Education* 25(1): 29-43.

Perteghella, Manuela and Eugenia Loffredo, eds. *Translation and Creativity: Perspectives on Creative Writing and Translation Studies.* London: Continuum, 2006.

Quarterly Literary Review Singapore. (2010) "About QLRS". [http://www.qlrs.com/about.asp.] Accessed 1.06.10.

Rogers, Kate. *City of Stairs.* Hong Kong: Haven Books, 2012.

Roth, Michael S. "Foucault's 'History of the Present'". *History and Theory* 20.1 (1981): 32-46.

Rubdy, Rani. "Creative Destruction: Singapore's Speak Good English Movement". *World Englishes* 20.3 (2001): 341-355.

Sartre, Jean-Paul. *The Imaginary: A Phenomenological Psychology of the Imagination.* Trans. Jonathan Webber. London: Routledge, 2004. [1940].

---. *What is Literature?* Trans. Bernard Frechtman. New York: Philosophical Library, 1949.

Scott, Clive. *Street Photography: From Atget to Cartier-Bresson.* New York: I. B. Tauris, 2007.

Shaull, Richard. "Foreword". Paulo Freire. *Pedagogy of the Oppressed.* New York; London: Continuum, 2005. [1970]

Simmel, Georg. *The Sociology of George Simmel.* Trans. Kurt H. Wolff. Illinois: The Free Press, 1950.

---. *The View of Life: Four Metaphysical Essays with Journal Aphorisms.* Trans. John A. Y. Andrews and Donald N. Levine. Chicago: The University of Chicago, 2010.

Slavick, Madeleine Marie. *Delicate Access.* Hong Kong: Sixth Finger Press, 2004.

Sontag, Susan. *On Photography.* New York: Picador, 1973.

Tay, Eddie. *A Lover's Soliloquy.* Hong Kong: Sixth Finger Press, 2005.

---. *Dreaming Cities.* Singapore: Math Paper Press, 2016.

---. *Remnants.* Singapore: Ethos Books, 2001.

---. *The Mental Life of Cities.* Hong Kong: Chameleon Press, 2010.

---. "Unsettling Ways of Exile: The Unhomely in the Poetry of Wong Phui Nam". C. Sankaran, L.-G. Leong and R. S. Patke, eds. *Complicities: Connections and Divisions.* Bern, Switzerland: Peter Lang, 2003. 179-188.

Teng, Qian Xi. "Three Love Objects". *Quarterly Literary Review Singapore* 5.4 (2006). [http://www.qlrs.com/poem.asp?id=534] Accessed 10.7.08.

Thrift, Nigel. "Space: The Fundamental Stuff of Geography". *Key Concepts in Geography*. 2nd ed. Eds. Nicholas J. Clifford, Sarah L. Holloway, Stephen P. Rice and Gill Valentine. London: SAGE, 2009. 85-96.

Thumboo, Edwin. *A Third Map: New and Selected Poems*. Singapore: UniPress, 1993.

---. "Introduction". Thumboo (ed) *The Second Tongue: An Anthology of Poetry from Singapore and Malaysia*. Singapore: Heinemman, 1976. vii-xxxv.

---. *Still Travelling*. Singapore: Ethos, 2008.

Thumboo, Edwin et. al, eds. Words for the 25th: *Readings by Singapore Writers*. Singapore: UniPress, 1990.

Toh Hsien Min. *Means to an End*. Singapore: Landmark Books, 2008.

Tung, Peter, Raymond Lam and Wai King Tsang. "English as a Medium of Instruction in Post-1997 Hong Kong: What Students, Teachers, and Parents Think". *Journal of Pragmatics* 28 (1997): 441-459.

Van Manen, Max. "Phenomenology of Practice". *Phenomenology & Practice*, Volume 1.1 (2007): 11-30.

Wagner, Tamara S. "Boutique multiculturalism and the Consumption of Repulsion: Re-disseminating Food Fictions in Malaysian and Singaporean Diasporic Novels". *Journal of Commonwealth Literature* 42.1 (2007): 31–46.

Wong, Phui. Nam. *Ways of Exile: Poems from the First Decade*. London: Skoob, 1993.

Wong, Jennifer. *Summer Cicadas*. Hong Kong: Chameleon, 2006.

Writers' Centre Norwich. "Alvin Pang – Candles". [http://www.youtube.com/watch?v=iyWEdu3I-5A]. YouTube video. Uploaded 22 June 2012. Accessed 6 June 2014.

Xu, Xi. *Evanescent Isles: From My City-Village*. Hong Kong: Hong Kong UP, 2008.

Yap, Arthur. *Commonplace*. Singapore: Heinemann Educational Books (Asia), 1977.

---. *Down the Line*. Singapore: Heinemann Educational Books, 1980.

---. *Man Snake Apple & Other Poems*. Singapore : Heinemann Asia, 1986.

---. *Only Lines*. [Singapore]: Federal Publications, [1971].

---. *The Space of City Trees*. London: Skoob, 2000.

Yong, Shu Hoong. *Frottage*. Singapore: Firstfruits, 2005.